BRASS ENSEMBLE
METHOD
FOR
MUSIC EDUCATORS

Jay D. Zorn
University of Southern California

WADSWORTH PUBLISHING COMPANY, INC.
BELMONT, CALIFORNIA

To Eva and Mark, Mimi and Lisa

Book production by MUSIC-BOOK ASSOCIATES, INC., New York City

Printed in the United States of America

2 3 4 5 6 7 8 9 10—81 80 79 78 77

Library of Congress Cataloging in Publication Data

Zorn, Jay D
    Brass ensemble method for music educators.

    Bibliography: p. 170
    Includes index.
    1. Brass instruments—Methods. I. Title.
MT339.2.Z   788'.01'0712   76-57673
ISBN 0-534-00503-9

Acknowledgments for Music Examples

Belwin-Mills Publishing Corp.:

    Cornet Solo, *Prelude* by Henry Johnson (pp. 99-103), copyright 1957, Belwin
    Inc. Reprinted by permission of Belwin Inc.

    Canzona by Vladimir Bakaleinikoff (pp. 104-110), copyright 1939, Belwin Inc.
    Reprinted by permission of Belwin Inc.

    Recitative and Romance by A. Louis Scarmolin (pp. 111-114), copyright 1955,
    Belwin Inc. Reprinted by permission of Belwin Inc.

    Bordogni Medley by Marco Bordogni, arr. by Richard W. Bowles (pp. 115-118),
    copyright 1973, Belwin-Mills. Reprinted by permission of Belwin-Mills.

EDITOR'S FOREWORD

Instruction in instruments is an important part of the training of future instrumental music teachers. Part of their future success as teachers depends on their knowledge of instruments other than their major instrument. Learning "minor" or "secondary" instruments has two parts. One is a basic ability in playing the instrument—fingerings, embouchure, playing position, and so on. The other part is a knowledge of how to teach the instrument to students at the beginning and intermediate levels. These two aspects of instruction in instruments are by no means contradictory. However, sometimes students in such classes or lessons concentrate almost exclusively on learning to play the instrument, which leaves them deficient in teaching knowledge. In other cases, such instruction contains little playing of music, and therefore the learning that results is largely a "head" knowledge based on limited practical understanding.

The WADSWORTH SERIES IN CLASS INSTRUMENTAL METHODS seeks to bring together the best of both the playing and teaching sides of the secondary instrumental instruction. These books contain material for the future instrumental teachers to learn to play. There is also information about how to teach the instrument to beginning students.

The WADSWORTH SERIES books are basically ensemble methods books. Since there is seldom time in undergraduate music-education curriculums for instruction on individual instruments, like instruments are learned at the same time in the same class. Because of the variety of instruments available, more interesting music can be performed.

Brass Ensemble Method for Music Educators by Jay Zorn of the University of Southern California was selected for inclusion in the WADSWORTH SERIES IN CLASS INSTRUMENTAL METHODS because it is an ensemble method, and includes information about teaching as well as material to play. Equally as significant, however, it is a tested class brass-methods textbook by an experienced teacher of such courses. The material is designed specifically with the college secondary-instrumental students in mind. The explanations are brief and to-the-point, and the music is interesting and challenging to music majors. In short, it is well suited to meet the needs of a brass course for future instrumental-music teachers.

Charles R. Hoffer
Indiana University

PREFACE

The purpose of this book is to enable prospective music teachers to further develop basic performance skills and understandings so that they can effectively teach brass instruments to their students.

Integral to this method is the brass-ensemble format which affords students in the brass-methods-class the opportunity to perform brass chamber-ensemble music and ensemble studies. The brass ensemble has proven itself to be an extremely effective vehicle through which to explore musical balance, phrasing, timbre, intonation, styles, and other performance concepts. Furthermore, the brass-ensemble format is practical as it makes only modest demands upon an institution's instrument inventory. An ideal class of twelve, for instance, requires only three trumpets, three horns, three trombones, two baritone horns, and one tuba to meet the needs of the class for the entire semester.

The first chapter on Beginning Instruction covers the basic material a college methods-class student needs for his first class session on each brass instrument. Though each instrument is started individually, it is recommended that all students be present to observe the typical problems encountered by beginning brass players. The built-in redundancy that results from examining the beginner's problems with each change of instrument should aid the prospective teachers to teach their beginning brass students.

The second chapter on Brass Ensemble Developmental Studies and Chamber Music Ensemble Rounds is designed to be started in the second class session and continued throughout the duration of each instrument's study. Beginning with Developmental Study No. 15, each class session should supplement the developmental studies with pieces from the third chapter on Brass Chamber Music Ensemble Selections.

The Brass Chamber Music Ensemble Selections in Chapter 3, compositions by Bach, Luther, Tallis, Susato, Pezel, Reiche, Palestrina, Beethoven, Purcell, Glazounov and others, were carefully chosen and graded to provide a musical challenge that does not overtax the student's limited performing skills and endurance. Most of the selections were originally composed for brass instruments and needed only minor transcribing for the brass-methods-class quintet of instruments.

The recital solos with piano accompaniment may be used in a number of ways. They may be performed in class to discuss common brass-performance problems peculiar to playing with piano accompaniment. They may also be used as a final performance test on each of the brass instruments—a sort of individual final project.

Two chapters of discussion material on Brass Instruments Performance Concepts and Teaching Brass Instruments in the Schools appear toward the end of the book. They are important and should not be neglected. Since beginning brass players require periodic rests from playing, there is always time in every class session to incorporate this discussion material. Though many students will also take a course on the Teaching of Instrumental Music— indeed, I teach this course at our university—I have found that the discussion material contained in these two chapters is better dealt with while the student is experiencing the actual problems of learning a brass instrument.

It is my hope that students and instructors will find the performance material satisfying and the discussion material practical and relevant and that it will inspire them to assist in raising the performance level and enjoyment of the young brass musicians in our schools.

I would like to thank the fine students at the University of Southern California School of Music for their valuable assistance in preparing this book. Thanks are due to Charles Hoffer of Indiana University, whose encouragement and editorial suggestions were needed and appreciated. A special gratitude is extended to some of my former brass teachers, colleagues, and friends, whose ideas also appear here, especially: Robert Marsteller, William Vacchiano, John Ware, Mitchel Jellen, John Clyman, Carl "Doc" Severinsen, and Phil Farkas. I would also like to thank the following reviewers for their comments: Terry Applebaum, Northwestern University; Wilbur England, Indiana University; and Frederick Fairchild, University of Illinois, Urbana. I alone, of course, am responsible for any possible errors or omissions.

Jay Zorn

SUGGESTED CLASS SEQUENCE FOR USING THE BRASS ENSEMBLE FOR MUSIC EDUCATORS*

Class One

Assign instruments.
Chapter 1—all.

Student assignment. Chapter 1—all.
Memorize fingering and position chart.

Class Two

Chapter 2—Studies, Nos. 1—8 (repeat as necessary). Rounds, Nos. 9, 10.
Chapter 5—five to ten minute discussion.
Chapter 3—Selection, No. 1.

Student assignment. Chapter 2—Studies and Rounds, Nos. 1—14.

Class Three

Chapter 2—Studies and Rounds, Nos. 1—14.
Chapter 5—five to ten minute discussion.
Chapter 3—Selections, Nos. 1—4.

Student assignment. Chapter 2—Studies and Rounds, Nos. 1—20.
Chapter 3—Selections, Nos. 1—9.

Class Four

Chapter 2—Studies, Nos. 15—20.
Chapter 5 or Chapter 6—five to ten minute discussion.
Chapter 3—Selections, Nos. 5—9.

*The suggested sequence is for a traditional format of fifty-minute classes, two classes per week, fifteen-week semester or thirty fifty-minute classes.

Student assignment.   Chapter 2—Studies and Rounds, Nos. 1—25.
   Chapter 3—Selections, Nos. 10—15.
   Chapter 4—prepare solo.

Class Five

   Chapter 2—Studies and Rounds, Nos. 15—25 (without repeats).
   Chapter 5 or Chapter 6—five to ten minute discussion.
   Chapter 3—Selections, Nos. 10—15. Repeat any from Selections, Nos. 1—9.

Student assignment.   Chapter 2—Studies, Nos. 15—30.
   Chapter 3—Selections, Nos. 10—15.
   Chapter 4—Prepare solo with piano accompaniment.

Class Six

   Chapter 2—Studies, Nos. 21—30.
   Chapter 5 or Chapter 6—five to ten minute discussion.
   Chapter 3—Selections, Nos. 16—18.

Student assignment.   Chapter 4—Solo with piano accompaniment.
   Appendix C.

Class Seven

   Individual Performance Examination (approximately four minutes for each student).
   Chapter 4—Solo with piano accompaniment (approximately two minutes of the solo).
   Appendix C—One octave chromatic scale and any two or three major or minor scales
      from memory.

Classes Eight to Fourteen
Classes Fifteen to Twenty-one
Classes Twenty-two to Twenty-seven

   Change instruments and repeat above sequence.

Classes Twenty-eight to Thirty

   Individual Performance Final Examination.
   Chapter 4—Entire solo with piano accompaniment.

CONTENTS

Chapter 1

BEGINNING INSTRUCTION

BREATHING

Breath control is an extremely important function in brass-instrument performance, as important as the use of the bow is in string-instrument performance. The breath not only supplies the energy to vibrate the lips, but also directly affects tone quality, range, endurance, and nearly all other elements of brass-instrument performance. Therefore, the study of a brass instrument should begin with an examination of the breathing process.

Normal breathing, though adequate for everyday activities, is not sufficient for brass-instrument performance. A more exaggerated breathing is required for the air to push against the resistance of the embouchure-mouthpiece-instrument combination.

The production of breath support for brass-instrument performance can be viewed as a three-fold process: (1) inhalation, (2) switchover, and (3) exhalation.

Inhalation

In taking a deep breath for brass-instrument performance, the muscles of the diaphragm contract downward while the rib cage expands outward (Figure 1).

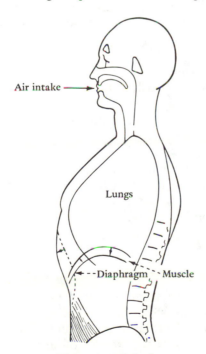

Figure 1. Inhalation.

The following experiments are vital to the understanding of the inhalation process.

EXPERIMENT: Examining the muscles used in the inhalation. Take a slow, deep inhalation as though you were sipping through a straw and notice how your rib cage and abdomen expand. Repeat the experiment if necessary.

Was your inhalation as full as possible? To find out, try the next experiment.

EXPERIMENT: Exploring inhalation capacity. Again, take a slow, sipping inhalation. When your lungs feel full to capacity, hold your breath for a second, then sip in still more air.

This experiment should give you an idea of your inhalation capacity. It was probably a good deal more than you anticipated and dramatically more than a normal, everyday-activity breath intake. It should be pointed out, however, that this sort of double inhalation is not recommended for performance, but is useful as an experiment. Your ultimate goal is to take in as much air as possible with a single inhalation.

Switchover

There is a quick change in the breathing process between inhalation and exhalation. It is a slight pause and setting of the abdominal muscles around the waist just before exhalation that this author calls the *switchover*.

EXPERIMENT: Analyzing the switchover. Take a slow, sipping inhalation. When your lungs are full, hold everything for several seconds, and note that a new set of muscles has taken over control to hold the air from rushing out. This is the *switchover*.

Exhalation

In the exhalation process, the abdominal muscles surrounding the waist control the rate and pressure of the air being exhaled. The process can be understood best through the following experiments:

EXPERIMENT: Analyzing the muscles controlling the exhalation. Take a moderate inhalation, make the switchover, and then simulate several coughs. Notice which muscles are being activated.

EXPERIMENT: Analyzing the rate and pressure of the exhaled air. Take a slow, full inhalation, make the switchover, and then exhale gradually, sounding the sibilant, "Sssss..." Try varying the loudness level of the sibilant.

Repeat this final experiment several times until you thoroughly understand the whole breathing process.

Eventually, adequate control of the breathing process becomes automatic, but in the beginning the brass-instrument student needs to concentrate on his breathing. Poor tone quality, limited range, or lack of endurance are usually indications that the player's breathing process is not functioning adequately. When this occurs, the player should re-examine the preceding discussion and the experiments on breathing.

EMBOUCHURE BUZZ

The beginning brass-instrument player's first tones are produced by *buzzing*, that is, by vibrating the lips without the mouthpiece or instrument. To accomplish this the player moistens the lips slightly to make them more pliable, then forms an embouchure as shown in Figure 2, takes a deep inhalation, and, finally, releases a jet stream of air to the center of the lips allowing them to vibrate. The player should concentrate on keeping the muscles surrounding the lips firm, especially at the corners of the mouth.

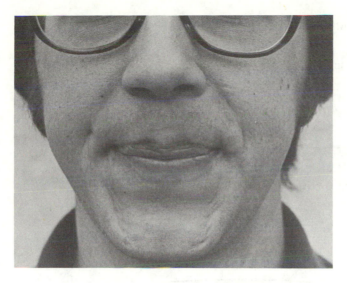

Figure 2. Forming an *embouchure*.

Ensemble Lip Buzzing Studies

Directions: Perform these studies using a lip buzz.

ENSEMBLE STUDY NO. 1. Lip Buzzing*

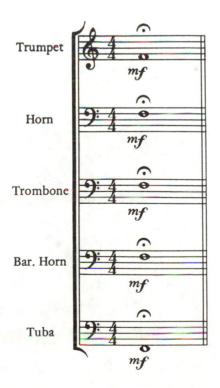

*These studies are written in concert pitch and are to sound as written. The instructor should sound the concert pitch first on the piano or another instrument to aid students in locating their pitches.

ENSEMBLE STUDY NO. 2. Lip Buzzing

Mouthpiece Placement

A mouthpiece placement method widely used and simple to remember is the following: the inside rim of every brass-instrument mouthpiece is placed on the player's lower lip line (Figure 3). The amount of upper lip encompassed by the rest of the mouthpiece will vary with both players and mouthpieces.

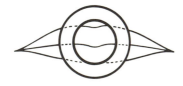

Figure 3. Mouthpiece placement.

Figure 4. Mouthpiece placement, side view.

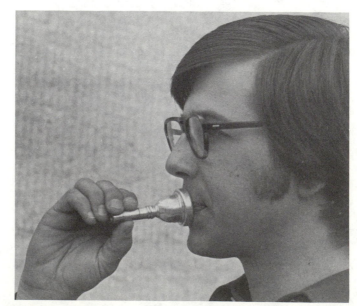

Figure 5. Trumpet/Cornet mouthpiece placement.

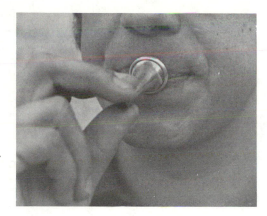

Figure 6. Horn mouthpiece placement.

Figure 7. Trombone/Baritone horn mouthpiece placement.

Figure 8. Tuba mouthpiece placement.

Ensemble Mouthpiece Studies

Directions: Perform this study with the mouthpiece.

ENSEMBLE STUDY NO. 3. Mouthpiece Study*

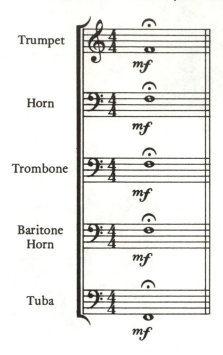

ENSEMBLE STUDY NO. 4. Mouthpiece Study

*These studies are written in concert pitch and are to sound as written. The instructor should sound the concert pitch first on the piano or another instrument to aid students in locating their pitches.

ENSEMBLE STUDY NO. 5. Mouthpiece Study

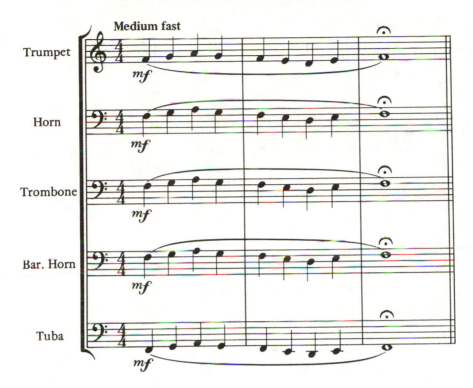

Beginning Tonguing*

The beginning brass performer needs to be concerned with tones that are either slurred or tongued. The slurred passages require an articulation only at the start of the passage. The articulated tones are produced when the tongue, acting as a release valve, lets air through to vibrate the lips.

Legato tonguing.   The placement of the tongue is the same that the player would use to pronounce the syllable *doo*.† This produces a legato articulation which is preferred for most brass playing.

After the start of a series of *doos* (legato tonguings), the tongue only slightly interrupts the flow of air. The action is similar to a finger touching a stream of water from a hose just lightly enough to produce a bobble in the stream, similar to the following:

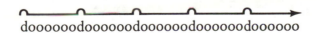

doooooodoooooodoooooodoooooodoooooo

Stopping the tone.   To stop a tone, the flow of air from the breath is stopped. The player should be careful not to stop the tone with the tongue, as in "*dood.*" This stops the tone too abruptly.

Legato Tonguing Studies

The following studies should be performed with the mouthpiece using legato tonguing throughout.

---

*A more detailed discussion of articulation appears on pp. 125-127.

†The lower brass instruments generally use a *daaw*, rather than a *doo*, pronunciation.

ENSEMBLE STUDY NO. 6. Legato Articulation with Mouthpiece Only*

ENSEMBLE STUDY NO. 7. Legato Articulation with Mouthpiece Only

*These studies are written in concert pitch and are to sound as written. The instructor should sound the concert pitch first on the piano or another instrument to aid students in locating their pitches.

8

ASSEMBLING THE BRASS INSTRUMENTS

Assembling a brass instrument is a relatively simple and obvious procedure. However, observing a few precautions may help to prevent potential damage to the instrument.

Care must be taken in getting the instrument out of its case. Damage often occurs when a student attempts to assemble an instrument with the case on his or her lap. The instrument can fall out of the case easily, or the top of the case can fall back while the instrument is being taken out of the case. To prevent this, the case should be placed on a solid, flat object such as the floor or a large table. Then, the player can use one hand to guide the instrument out of the case while holding the case lid back with the other.

The mouthpiece should always be assembled on the instrument last, and only when the player has a firm grip on the instrument. The mouthpiece should be *gently* screwed into the mouthpiece receiver. *It should never be tapped or struck* because the brass is soft and will spread. This may cause the mouthpiece to get stuck necessitating the use of a mouthpiece puller to free it.

Assembling a trombone involves a special problem, since the trombone consists of three parts: the bell section, the slide section, and the mouthpiece. After opening the case, the player should first check the slide lock to see that it is secure. Next, the player should grasp the bell section with the left hand, keeping the bell pointed to the floor. Then, with the right hand, the player should take hold of the slide section and bring it up to fit with the bell section also securing the joining screw. Finally, with the instrument held in the left hand, the player can remove the mouthpiece from the case with the right hand.

HOLDING AND PLAYING THE INSTRUMENTS

Trumpet/Cornet

Left-hand position.   Four fingers of the left hand are placed over the third valve slide with the *ring* finger placed in the third valve ring. The palm and thumb grip the valve casings as in Figure 9.

Figure 9. Trumpet/Cornet left-hand position.

Right-hand position.   The thumb of the right hand is placed between the first and second valve casings just below the leadpipe. The tips of the fingers are placed on the valve tips (Figure 10).

9

Figure 10. Trumpet/Cornet right-hand position.

Horn

Left-hand position. The horn's valves are operated by the fingers of the left hand. Most horns are equipped with both a thumb grip and a little finger grip (Figure 11).

Figure 11. Horn left-hand position.

*It is recommended that the instructor play the starting tones on the piano or another instrument to help students in locating their pitches.

Right-hand position.   The right hand is slightly cupped (Figure 12).
   The cupped hand is inserted into the bell of the horn (Figure 13). This allows for convenient changes in the shape of the hand to accommodate for changes in tone quality as well as pitch.

Figure 12. Horn right-hand cupped position.

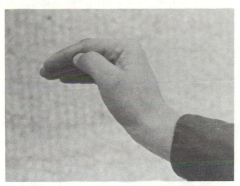

Figure 13. Right hand inserted into the bell.

Bell angle.   The bell of the horn is angled away from the player's body so that the tone will not be blocked. Some players advocate placing the rim of the bell on the player's inner thigh; others place the rim on the outside of the thigh or entirely off the leg as in Figure 14.

Figure 14. Bell angle.

INDIVIDUAL STUDY: Horn Starting Tones with Instrument*

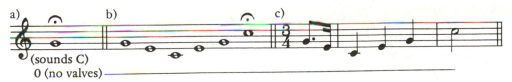

(sounds C)
0 (no valves)

*It is recommended that the instructor play the starting tones on the piano or another instrument to help students in locating their pitches.

Trombone

Left-hand position.   The first finger of the left hand is extended over the mouthpiece or mouthpiece shank. The thumb grips the cross brace of the bell, while the other three fingers grip around the slide's upper cross brace (Figure 15).

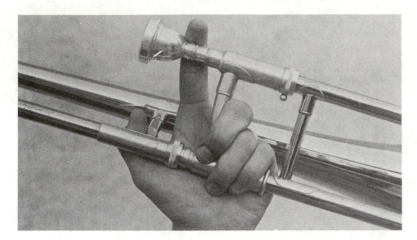

Figure 15. Trombone left-hand position.

Right-hand position.   The right hand manipulates the slide, holding it at the cross with the thumb and two fingers as shown in Figure 16.

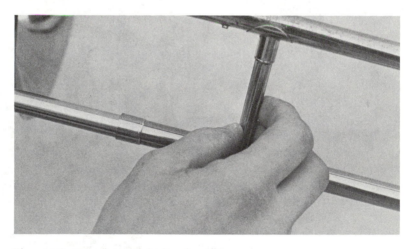

Figure 16. Trombone right-hand position.

INDIVIDUAL STUDY: Trombone Starting Tones with Instrument*

1 (1st position)

*It is recommended that the instructor play the starting tones on the piano or another instrument to help students in locating their pitches.

Baritone Horn

Left-hand position. The left arm comes around and cradles the instrument, while the left hand grips the third valve slide or the bell extension tubing (Figure 17).

Right-hand position. The right hand is rounded with the thumb placed in the thumb ring and the fingertips placed on the tips of the valves (Figure 17).

Figure 17. Baritone holding position.

INDIVIDUAL STUDY: Baritone Starting Tones with Instrument*

0 (no valves) ——————————————

---

*It is recommended that the instructor play the starting tones on the piano or another instrument to help students in locating their pitches.

Tuba

Left-hand position. Most of the tuba's weight rests on the player's chair between the legs, or on the inner thighs. The left hand grips any tubing that aids in balancing the instrument (Figure 18).

Right-hand position. The right hand is usually provided with a ring or grip for the thumb. The fingertips are placed on the tips of the valves (Figure 18).

Figure 18. Tuba holding position.

INDIVIDUAL STUDY: Tuba Starting Tones with Instrument*

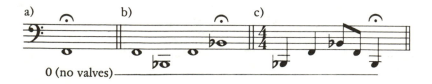

*It is recommended that the instructor play the starting tones on the piano or another instrument to help students in locating their pitches.

14

Sousaphone

Left-hand position.   The sousaphone balances mainly on the player's left shoulder and is supported by the left hand holding the bell extension tubing (Figure 19).

Right-hand position.   As with the tuba, the thumb is placed in a thumb grip or ring, and the fingertips are placed on the tips of the valves (Figure 19).

Figure 19. Sousaphone holding position.

ENSEMBLE STUDY NO. 8

Directions: The entire study can be played with first position for trombone and without valves for the other brass instruments.

16

Using the Valves and Slides

The function of valves and slides on brass instruments is to add tubing to the basic instrument, subsequently lowering the instrument's harmonic series.* For instance, by adding the second valve on the trumpet the entire harmonic series is lowered from a concert B♭ to a concert A (a minor second). Thus, the second valve has the effect of lowering any harmonic by a minor second.

Every brass-instrument performer should memorize the following chart along with the harmonic series for his or her instrument. Once the harmonic series is known, any fingering or slide position can be found.

Valve(s)	Slide Position	Interval Lowered	Step(s) Lowered
0	1	–	–
2	2	minor 2nd	½
1	3	major 2nd	1
12 (or 3)	4	minor 3rd	1½
23	5	major 3rd	2
13	6	perfect 4th	2½
123	7	augmented 4th	3

INDIVIDUAL PERFORMANCE STUDIES BASED ON THE DIATONIC AND CHROMATIC SCALES

Valved Instruments†

INDIVIDUAL STUDY: Trumpet/Cornet

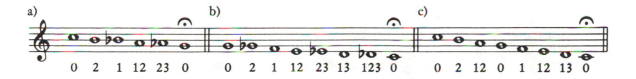

INDIVIDUAL STUDY: Horn

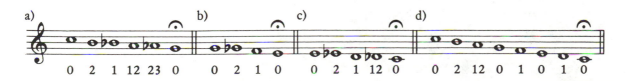

*Merely depressing valves or lengthening slides will not automatically result in a lower pitch. Players must vibrate their lips to match the new pitch; otherwise the added tubing will be added to a different partial and a different pitch will result. The interval lowered by the valve or slide combination will be consistent with the chart above, but will be from the wrong partial.

†Individual studies for the slide trombone will follow.

INDIVIDUAL STUDY: Baritone Horn

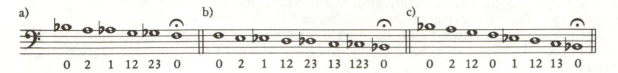

a)

0   2   1   12 23 0

b)

0   2   1   12 23 13 123 0

c)

0   2   12 0   1   12 13 0

INDIVIDUAL STUDY: Tuba

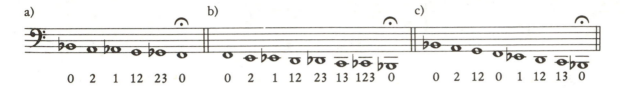

a)

0   2   1   12 23 0

b)

0   2   1   12 23 13 123 0

c)

0   2   12 0   1   12 13 0

Trombone Slide

INDIVIDUAL STUDY: Trombone

There are seven basic slide positions on the tenor trombone, and most of them are difficult to locate. Four positions—1, 3, 4, and 6—have general reference points that aid in their location.

Position 1:   As shown in Figure 20, the slide is held against the mouthpiece brace.

Figure 20. Position 1.

Position 3: As shown in Figure 21, the slide's crossbrace is even with the flare of the bell.

Figure 21. Position 3.

Position 4: As shown in Figure 22, the slide's crossbrace is moved just beyond the bell.

Figure 22. Position 4.

Position 6: As shown in Figure 23, the right arm is extended fully in a comfortable position, without stretching (stretching will move the slide to position 7).

Figure 23. Position 6.

INDIVIDUAL STUDY: Trombone Basic Chromatic and Diatonic Scale*

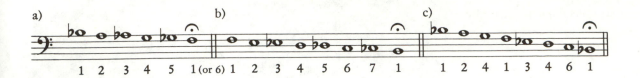

a) 1 2 3 4 5 1 (or 6)
b) 1 2 3 4 5 6 7 1
c) 1 2 4 1 3 4 6 1

ENSEMBLE STUDY NO. 9

Directions: On the conductor's cue, all perform the following chromatic scale patterns.†

a)   b)   c)

Trumpet
0 2 1 12 23 13 123   0 2 1 12 23 13 123   0 2 1 12 23 13 123
                           (0) (2)

Horn
0 2 1 12 23 13 123
    (0) (2)

Trombone
1 2 3 4 5 6 7   1 2 3 4 5 6 7   1 2 3 4 5 6 7

Bar. Horn
0 2 1 12 23 13 123   0 2 1 12 23 13 123   0 2 1 12 23 13 123
                           (0) (2)

Tuba
0 2 1 12 23 13 123   0 2 1 12 23 13 123   0 2 1 12 23 13 123
                           (0) (2)

Repeat faster

*Perform with a clear tone and secure intonation!

†The chromatic fingerings and slide positions shown above should be memorized and performed individually from any harmonic.

EXPANDED CHROMATIC-SCALE FINGERING AND SLIDE-POSITION CHARTS

The following charts contain all the fingerings and slide positions needed to perform any exercise or composition in this book. They should be memorized. More detailed charts appear in Appendix B for use in teaching.

Bb Trumpet/Cornet

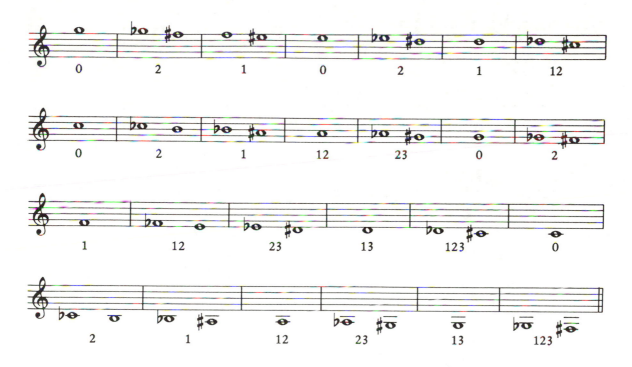

F Horn

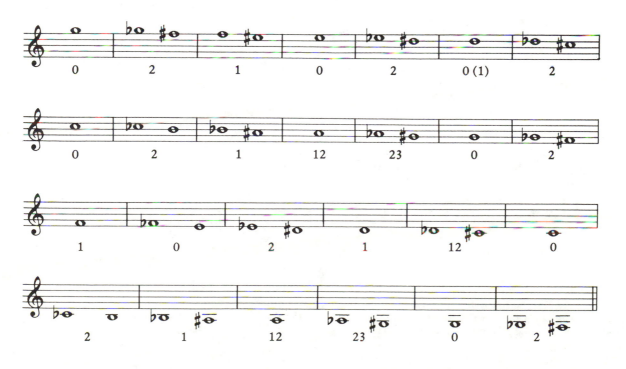

Trombone

Baritone Horn (four valves)*

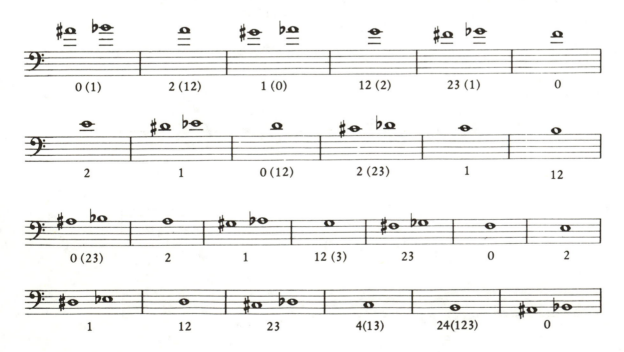

*Best fingerings are listed first. Fingerings in brackets are possible, but are generally poor in tone quality and intonation. More fingerings are possible in the upper register than appear here. The fourth valve is often found on intermediate and advanced student instruments and greatly aids in correcting some of the lower-register intonation problems.

BBb Tuba

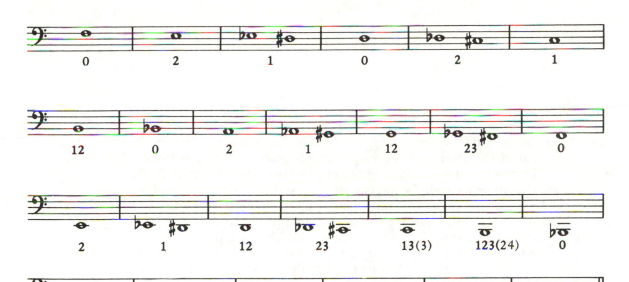

Chapter 2
BRASS ENSEMBLE DEVELOPMENTAL STUDIES AND CHAMBER MUSIC ENSEMBLE ROUNDS

DIRECTIONS FOR STUDY

Chapters 2 and 3 should be performed concurrently.* Each class session should be balanced by performing several of the Chapter 2 Developmental Studies and Rounds followed by several of the Chapter 3 Chamber Music Ensemble Selections. Half way through each class session five to ten minute discussions should be interspersed based upon material from Chapter 5, *Brass Instrument Performance Concepts,* and Chapter 6, *Teaching Brass Instruments in the Schools.* The discussion time will serve as a useful rest from performance as well as an effective means of exploring the important information covered in these chapters.

The Developmental Studies are intentionally concise and probably should be repeated often and at varying tempi. The two Advanced Studies from the Arban method should be considered optional material only within the capabilities of a few students.

---

*See Preface for a more detailed suggested sequence.

1. STUDY

2. STUDY

25

3. STUDY

4. STUDY

5. STUDY

6. STUDY

27

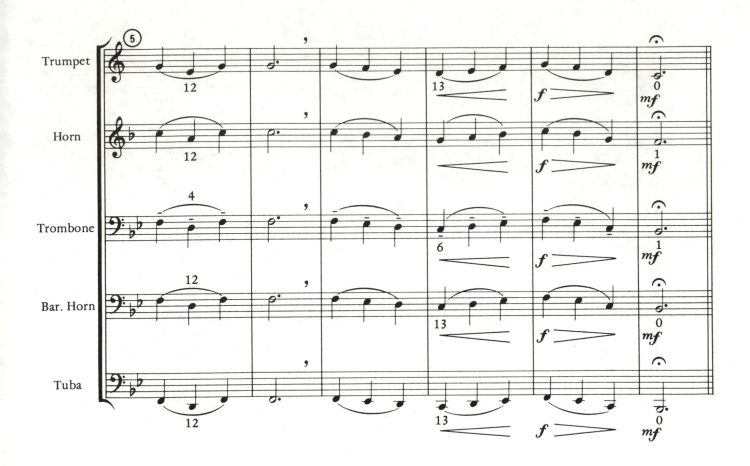

7. STUDY

8. STUDY

9. ROUND

Thomas Tallis
(c. 1505-1585)

29

10. THREE-PART ROUND

Anonymous

11. ROUND

Anonymous

12. STUDY

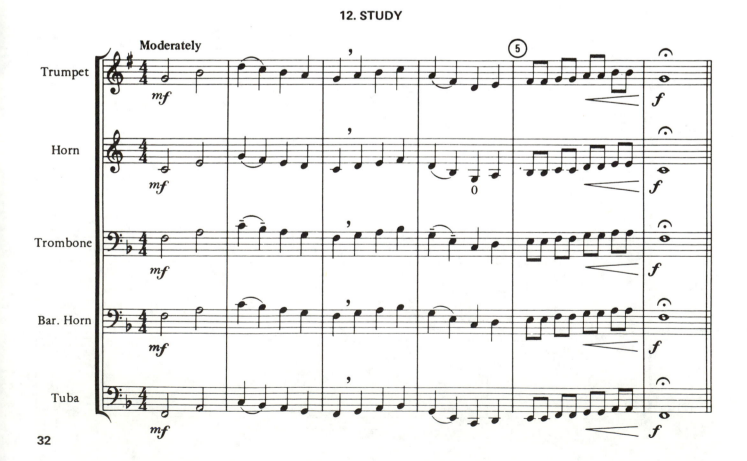

13. ROUND

Anonymous

34

Anonymous

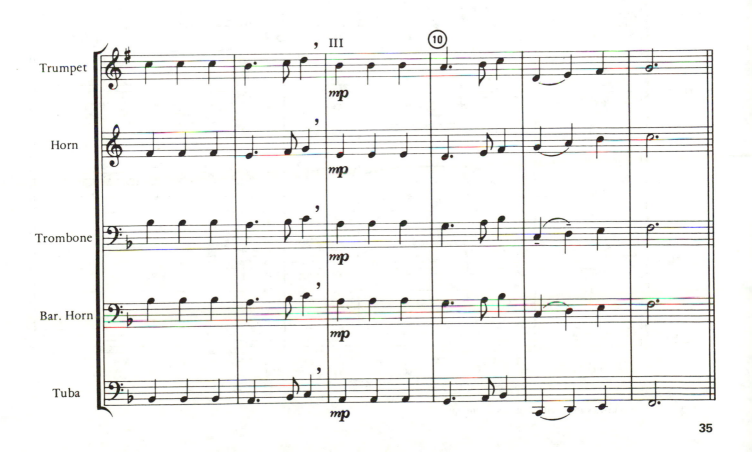

15. STUDY*

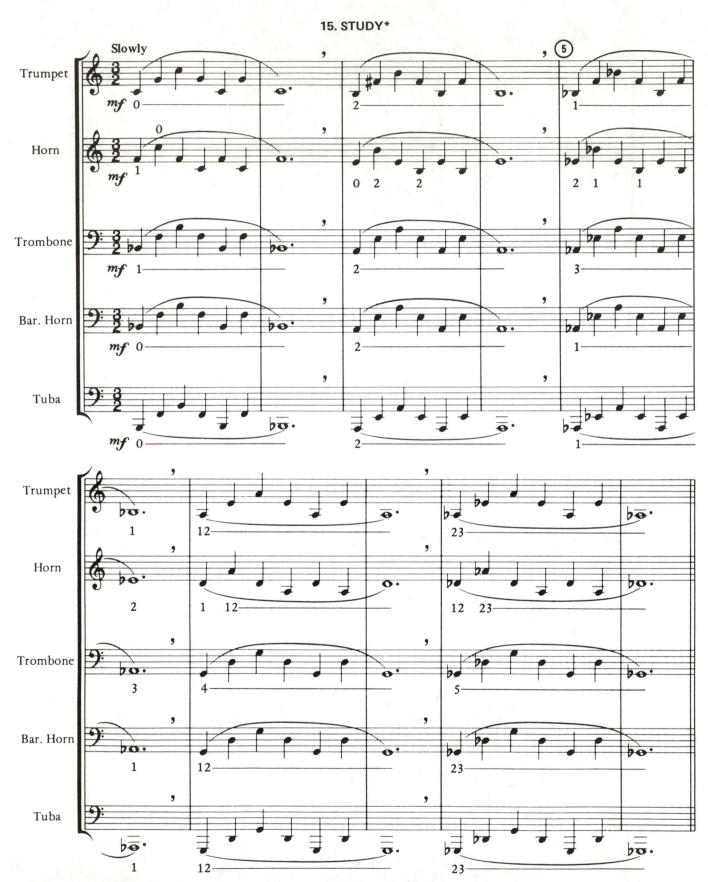

*This study also makes an excellent, quick warm up.

16. STUDY*

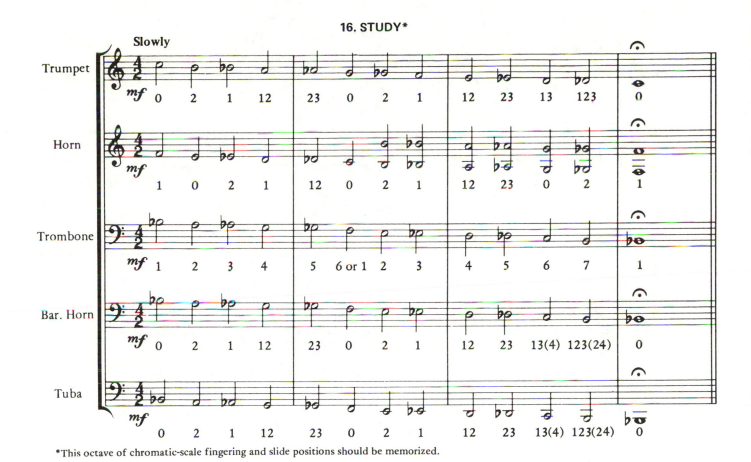

*This octave of chromatic-scale fingering and slide positions should be memorized.

17. STUDY

37

18. STUDY

19. STUDY

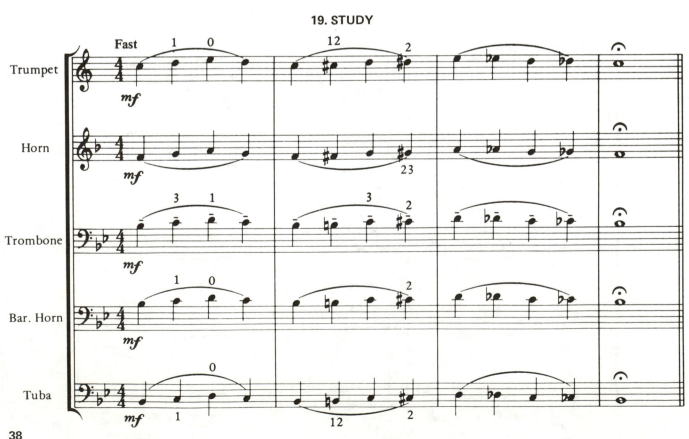

20. STUDY*

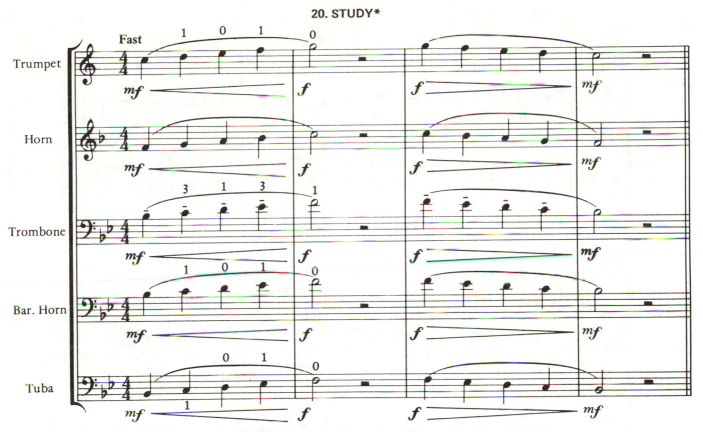

*See Chapter 5, p. 122 for a discussion of upper-register performance.

21. STUDY

22. STUDY

Directions: Play the preceding study with the following variations in articulation:

23. STUDY*

*Repeat faster.

24. STUDY

Directions: Play the preceding study with the following variations in articulation:

25. STUDY*

*Repeat faster.

26. STUDY

Directions: Play the preceding study with the following variations in articulation:

27. STUDY

Directions: Play the preceding study with the following variations in articulation:

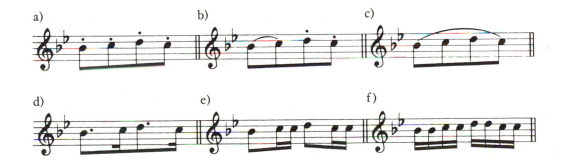

28. STUDY

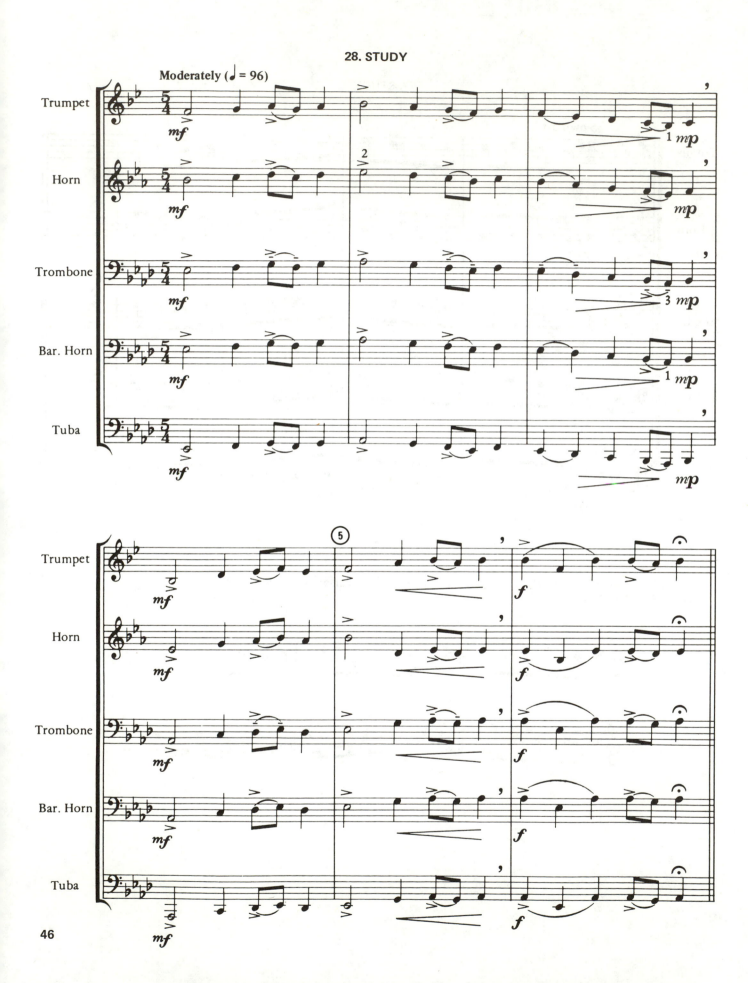

29. STUDY

47

30. STUDY

ADVANCED STUDY NO. 1: TONGUING

Arban (excerpt)

Moderately slow (♩. = 80)

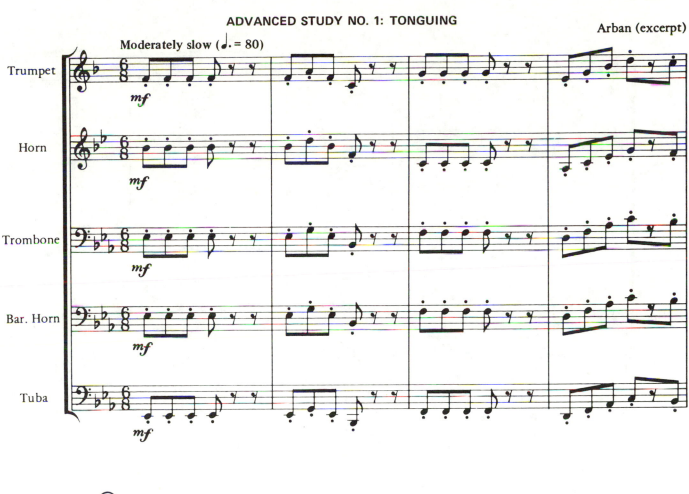

ADVANCED STUDY NO. 2: TONGUING

Arban (excerpt)

Chapter 3

BRASS CHAMBER MUSIC ENSEMBLE SELECTIONS

1. Louis Bourgeois, *Old Hundredth Hymn*
2. Tielman Susato, *Ronde for Instruments*
3. Ludwig van Beethoven, *Equali II,* Op. 195
4. Ludwig van Beethoven, *Equali III,* Op. 195
5. Nikolaus Ammerbach, *Passamezzo Antico,* "Saltarello"
6. Anonymous, *Chanson* from the "Attaingnant Collection"
7. Johann Sebastian Bach, *Chorale:* "Freu' Dich Sehr, O Meine Seele"
8. Claudin de Sermisy, *Chanson* from the "Attaingnant Collection"
9. John Addison, *Ayre*
10. Giovanni Palestrina, *O Bone Jesu*
11. Martin Luther/Bach, *Chorale:* "Ein' Feste Burg"
12. Gottfried Reiche, *Sonata No. 15*
13. Henry Purcell, *March* from "Funeral Music for Queen Mary II"
14. Henry Purcell, *Anthem* from "Funeral Music for Queen Mary II"
15. Henry Purcell, *Canzona* from "Funeral Music for Queen Mary II"
16. Johann Pezel, *Sonata No. 3*
17. Alexander Glazounov, *In Modo Religioso,* Op. 38
18. Jay Zorn, *Caccia for Brass Ensemble*

1. OLD HUNDREDTH HYMN

Louis Bourgeois
(c. 1510-c. 1561)

2. RONDE FOR INSTRUMENTS

Tielman Susato (Antwerp, 1551)
Arr. by Zorn

54

3. EQUALI II, OP. 195*

Ludwig van Beethoven (1770-1827)
Arr. by Zorn

*Originally scored for trombones.

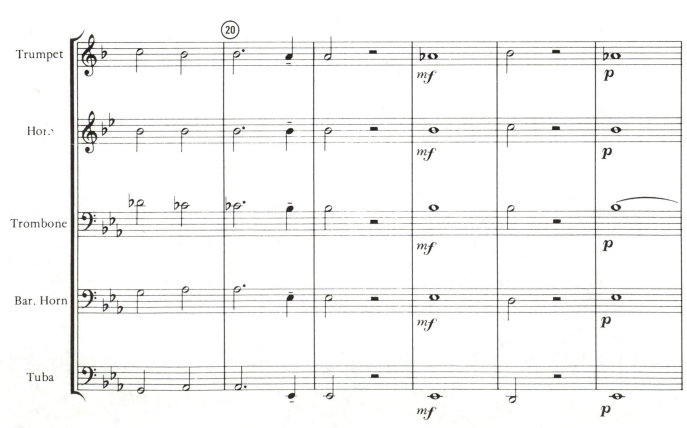

56

4. EQUALI III, OP. 195

Ludwig van Beethoven (1770-1827)
Arr. by Zorn

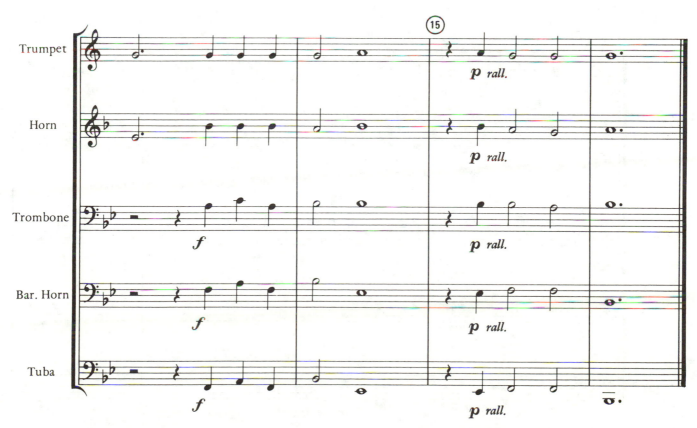

5. PASSAMEZZO ANTICO, "SALTARELLO"

Nikolaus Ammerbach (c. 1530-1597)
Arr. by Zorn

60

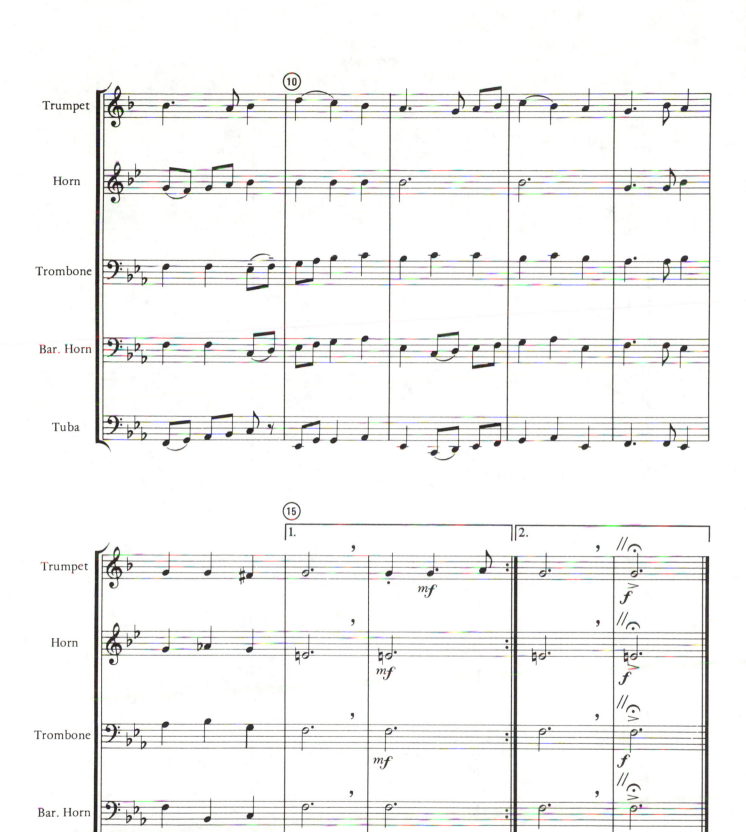

6. CHANSON
from the *Attaingnant Collection*

Anonymous (16th Cent.)
Arr. by Zorn

63

7. Chorale: FREU' DICH SEHR, O MEINE SEELE

Harmonized by J. S. Bach
(1685-1750)

64

8. CHANSON
from the *Attaingnant Collection*

Claudin de Sermisy (1531)
Arr. by Jay Zorn

67

9. AYRE

John Addison
(c. 1766-1844)

10. O BONE JESU

Giovanni Palestrina (1525-1594)
Arr. by Zorn

70

71

11. Chorale: EIN' FESTE BURG

Martin Luther (1529)
Harmonized by J. S. Bach

73

12. SONATA NO. 15

Gottfried Reiche
(1667-1734)

74

13. MARCH
from *Funeral Music for Queen Mary II*

Henry Purcell
(1658-1695)

14. ANTHEM
from *Funeral Music for Queen Mary II*

Henry Purcell
(1658-1695)

78

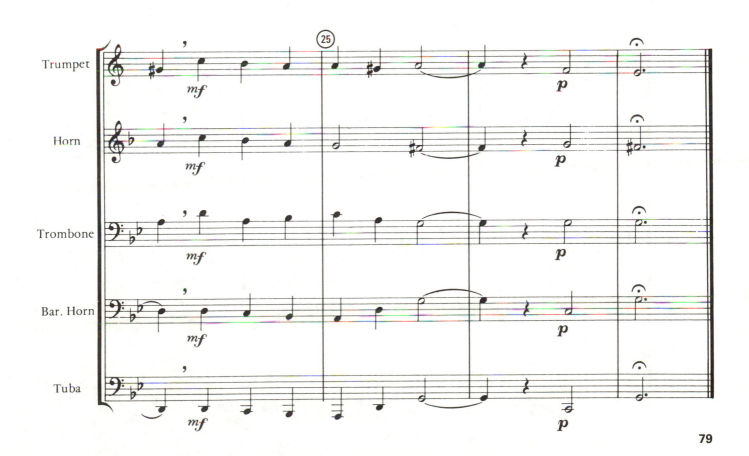

15. CANZONA
from *Funeral Music for Queen Mary II*

Henry Purcell
(1658-1695)

80

82

16. SONATA NO. 3

Johann Pezel
(1636-1694)

85

17. IN MODO RELIGIOSO, OP. 38

Alexander Glazounov
(1865-1936)

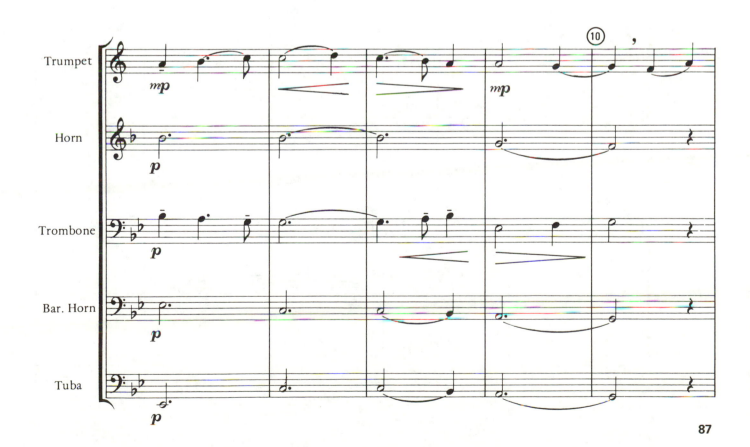

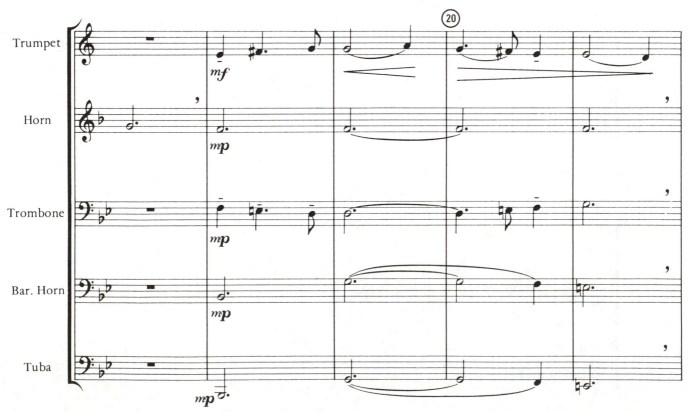

89

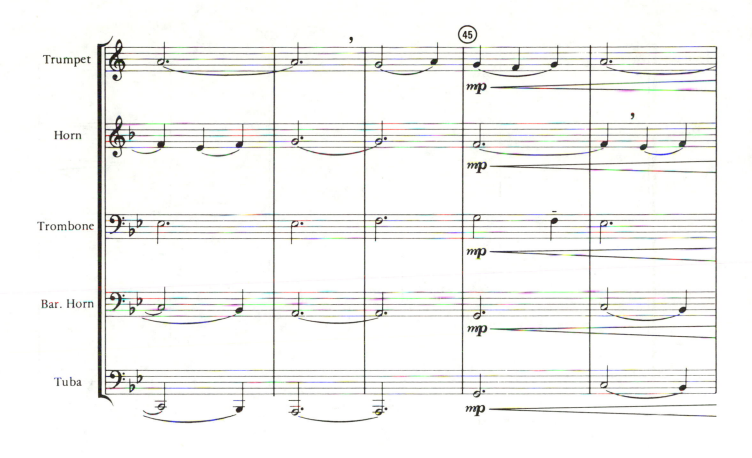

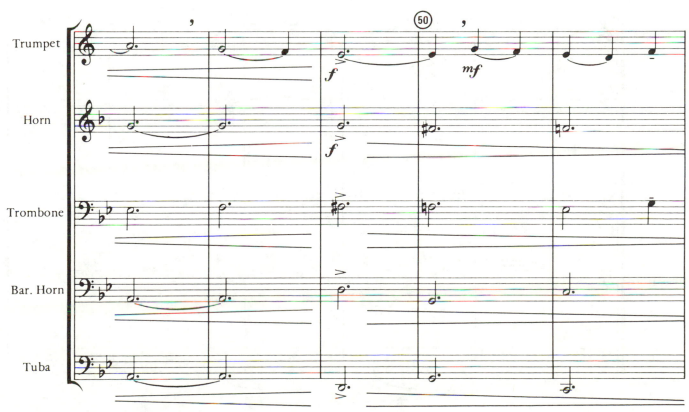

92

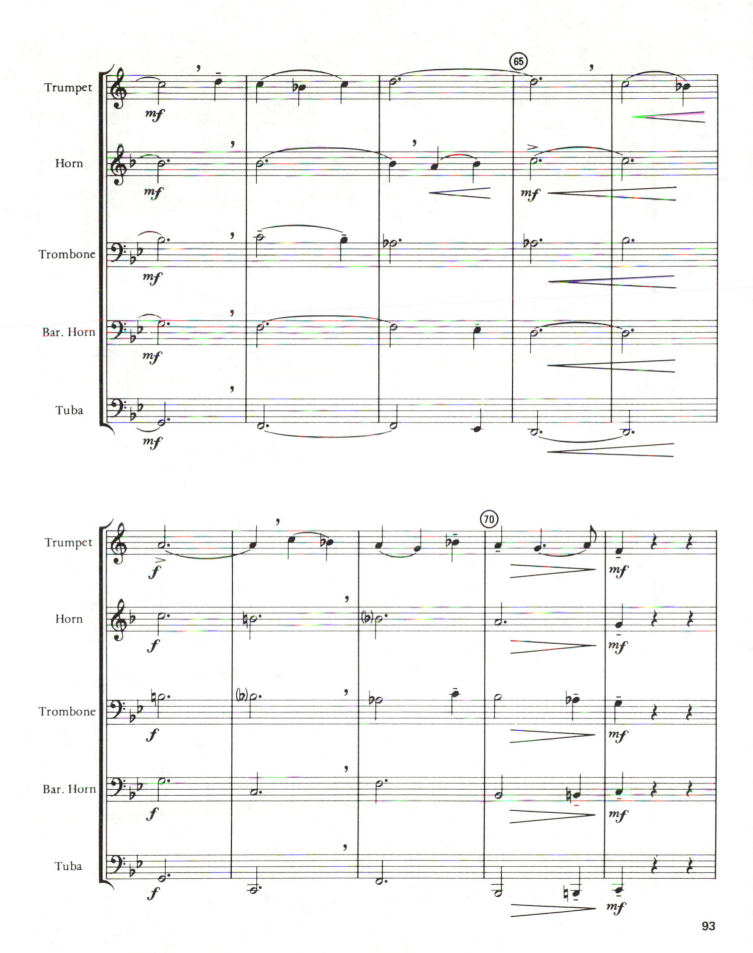

CACCIA FOR BRASS ENSEMBLE

Directions Prior to Performance:

1. The group chooses a short ostinato rhythm.

2. Each player performs the ostinato on a separate pitch that is selected randomly. The choice of pitches may be revised according to taste. In any case, the players should avoid traditional chords. Cluster type chords will be found to be the most effective.

3. Each player improvises a short "signature tune" or *leit motiv* that is characteristic of the instrument being performed. The tune should be memorized and brought out strongly during performance.

4. Each player gets out of his seat and selects a percussive sound from somewhere in the room. This sound may be continuously improvised during performance to suit the total composition.

5. Each performer sings a lyrical passage of his choice into his instrument. During performance this part should always be kept in the background.

6. One player is chosen to be the conductor.

Directions During Performance:

1. The conductor's role during performance is:
   a. to set the opening tempo with a downbeat
   b. to cue individual performers to enter at letter **B**
   c. to shape the dynamics and expression
   d. to indicate a cut off, hold, or fade out to end the piece.

2. All performers begin together at letter **A**, performing the chosen ostinato.

3. On cue one performer at a time begins performing the various sound events starting at letter **B**.

4. All performers keep repeating back to the sign at letter **B** until an ending is signaled by the conductor.

Sound Events Code:

(O) = OSTINATO   (P) = PERCUSSIVE SOUND

☆ S = SIGNATURE TUNE   (V) = VOCAL SOUND

⊔ = REST

CACCIA FOR BRASS ENSEMBLE (1975)

Jay Zorn

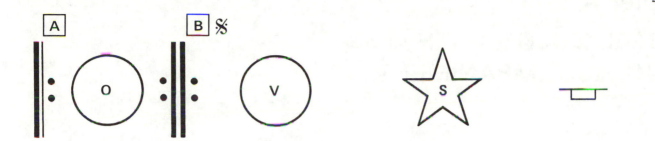

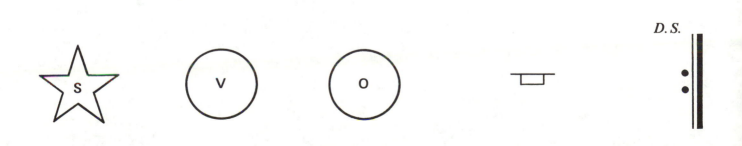

Chapter 4
RECITAL SOLOS WITH
PIANO ACCOMPANIMENT

1. **CORNET:**
   Henry Johnson, *Prelude*

2. **HORN:**
   Vladimir Bakaleinikoff, *Canzona*

3. **TROMBONE AND BARITONE HORN:**
   A. Louis Scarmolin, *Recitative and Romance*

4. **TUBA:**
   Marco Bordogni, *Bordogni Medley*. Arr. by Richard W. Bowles

PRELUDE

Solo B♭ Cornet

HENRY JOHNSON

99

PRELUDE
For B♭ Cornet and Piano

HENRY JOHNSON

Piano

101

A little faster (flowing)

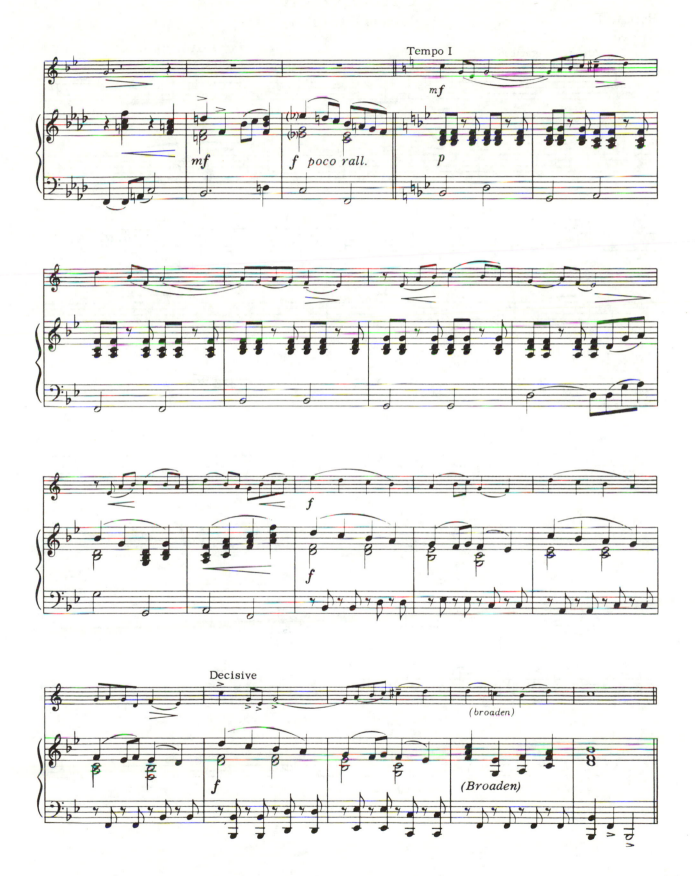

103

CANZONA
Horn in F and Piano

Horn in F

VLADIMIR BAKALEINIKOFF

CANZONA
Horn in F and Piano

Piano

VLADIMIR BAKALEINIKOFF

105

RECITATIVE AND ROMANCE

Solo for Trombone

A. LOUIS SCARMOLIN
A. S. C. A. P.

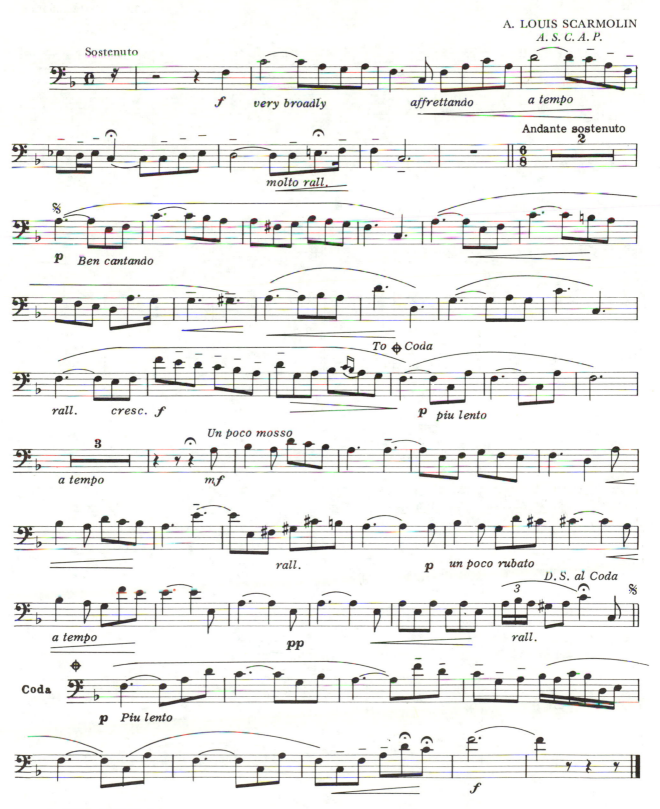

RECITATIVE AND ROMANCE

Solo for Trombone

A. LOUIS SCARMOLIN
A. S. C. A. P.

Piano

113

BORDOGNI MEDLEY

Tuba

Marco Bordogni (1788 - 1856) was a renowned voice teacher at the Paris Conservatory for more than thirty years. He composed many Vocalises which became popular not only as technical studies but also for their worth as music.

The BORDOGNI MEDLEY uses themes from two of these Vocalises.

Arr. by RICHARD W. BOWLES

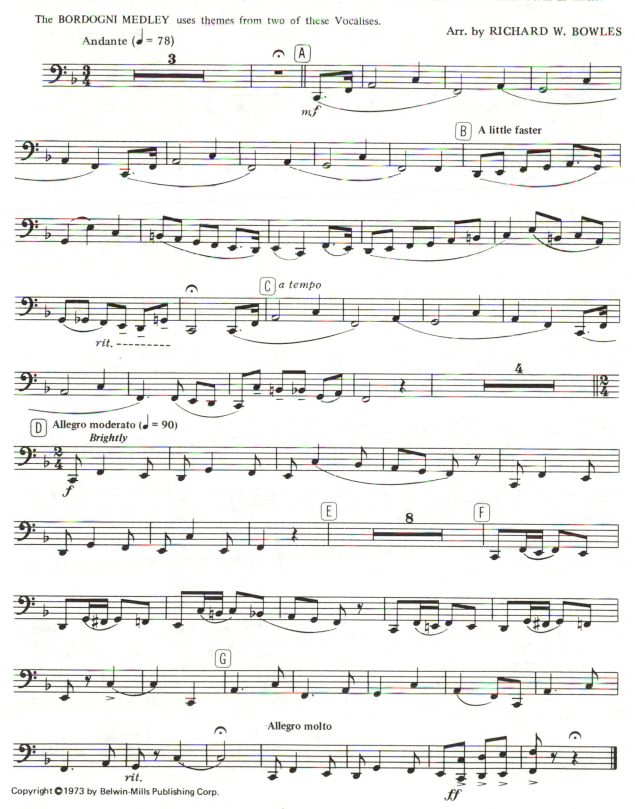

Piano

BORDOGNI MEDLEY

Arr. by RICHARD W. BOWLES

116

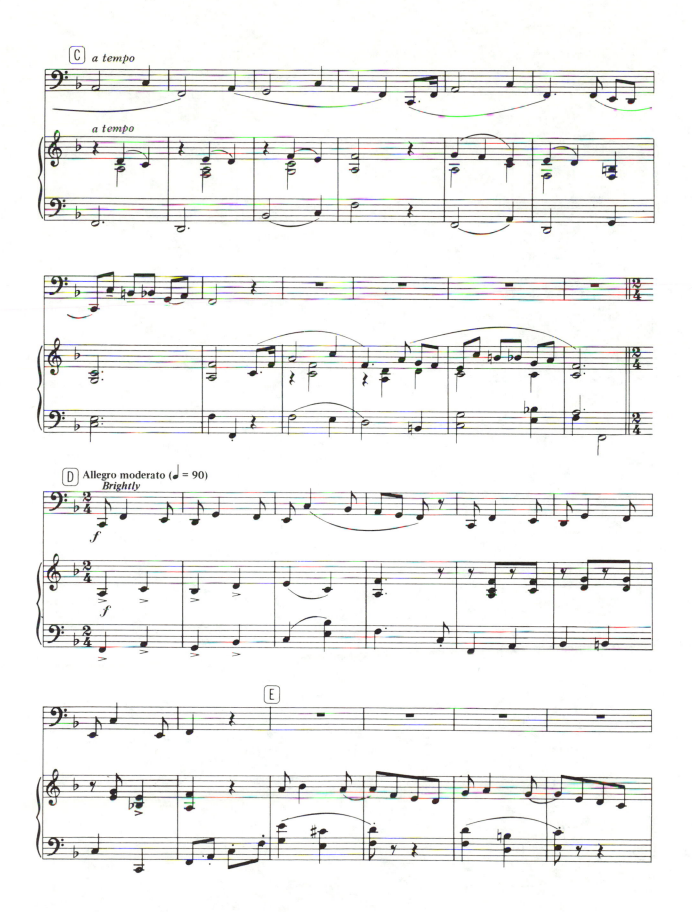

117

118

Chapter 5
BRASS INSTRUMENTS PERFORMANCE CONCEPTS

This chapter is devoted to basic concepts of brass-instrument performance a music educator needs to teach the brass instruments effectively at any level.

EMBOUCHURE

The ability of the lips to act as the vibrator in producing sounds on brass instruments is determined largely by the formation and tension of the lips, mouth, jaw, and facial muscles. The term for this formation in brass playing is *embouchure*, a French word that contains *bouche* meaning "mouth."

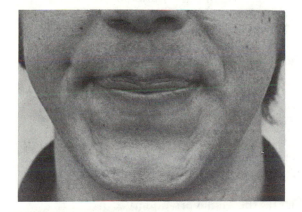

In forming an embouchure, the corners of the mouth and the muscles surrounding the lips are firmed as in Figure 24.

Figure 24. Forming an embouchure.

Aperture

The *aperture* is the opening between the lips and the surrounding surface of the lips that are set into vibration by the breath. The brass performer maintains a somewhat oval-shaped aperture, regardless of the size of the aperture. Figure 25 indicates a small-size aperture used mainly for trumpet and horn performance.

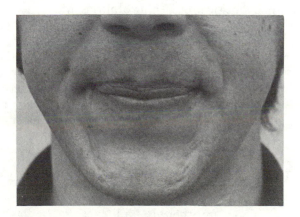

Figure 25. Small-size aperture.

By contrast, Figure 26 shows the large-size aperture required for tuba performance.

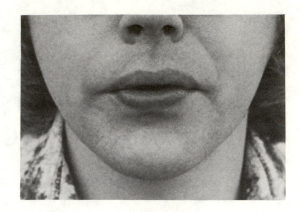

Figure 26. Large-size aperture.

Changing Pitches

Basically, two functions cause changes in pitch: lip tension and air pressure. Tensing the lips has the effect of raising the pitch, while relaxing lowers it. Increasing the air pressure without changing the size of the aperture causes the pitch to rise, while decreasing the air pressure lowers it.

Loudness Affects Aperture

In louder playing, more air is used and more lip-aperture surface vibrates. The greater increase in air pressure allows the aperture to enlarge while maintaining the same pitch. Therefore, a high pitch can be achieved softly by using a small lip aperture and moderate air pressure, or loudly by using a medium-size lip aperture and a great amount of air pressure. Of course, the choice is dictated most often by the actual music. However, when a player has a choice he or she should probably opt for increasing the air pressure in the upper register thus sparing the lip muscles from tiring. In any case, a brass player needs to develop both an *embouchure* and a *breathing* process.

BREATHING

As we have already seen, the breathing process used in brass-instrument performance is a three-fold process: (1) inhalation, (2) switchover, and (3) exhalation.

The lack of an adequate understanding of the breathing process is the most common problem for beginning and intermediate brass players. In general, these players underuse their physical breathing abilities. Most inexperienced players do not yet realize how much air is needed to play a brass instrument, and consequently do not take in sufficient air during their inhalation. This usually results in an unclear tone quality, difficulty in obtaining the upper register, short phrase lengths, and a short span of endurance.

Brass players' problems with breath support usually become noticeable when they attempt to perform in the upper register where several factors combine to create greater resistance: the air velocity speeds up, the oral cavity becomes smaller as the tongue is arched, the lip aperture gets smaller, the lips vibrate faster, and the air stream is more concentrated. All this requires the player to build up greater air pressure.

To develop a greater inhalation capacity the player should practice long, slow inhalations as outlined in the experiment on page 2.

Sustaining long tones on brass instruments is an excellent method for developing control of the whole breathing process. Timing the long tones with a stop watch adds a little element of fun to an otherwise dull exercise. In classes, students often enjoy timed long-tone contests.

A common mistake inexperienced players usually make is playing too softly on their brass instruments. The problem usually stems from playing in a large instrumental ensemble that has too many brass players. To keep the decibel count down directors usually insist that the brass players play at a consistently soft dynamic level. This not only inhibits the development of the players' optimum breathing capacities but also hinders their achieving a full tone quality as well. To counterbalance this problem, players should be advised to play louder during their home practice sessions than they do in the ensemble. Furthermore, since solo, chamber-music ensemble, and jazz ensemble performance usually benefit a brass-instrument performer's physical playing abilities more efficiently than the large instrumental ensembles, the developing brass player should be encouraged to engage in those modes of performance.

WARMING UP

The Olympic swimmer, the baseball player, and the musician all utilize carefully thought-out exercises to bring their coordination for performance quickly up to maximum. In playing a brass instrument, this warm-up is critical as it sets the quality of the performance that follows.

Each player needs to create his own "tailor-made" warm-up. A visit backstage to any major orchestra prior to a concert will find players warming up, each in his own way. No single warm-up will do for every instrument or every player.

The warm-up should be one that is easily memorized so that the player can begin each playing session by concentrating on the sound without being distracted by a printed page. Each player should keep the same warm-up and use it as sort of a gauge for measuring his or her performance condition at any given time. This will provide an indication of the weaknesses and strengths that will affect the performance that follows.

The following general format has been tried over a number of years and found to work extremely well for most brass players. With it a player or teacher can create an individual warm-up, or piece one together from several method books.

General Warm-up Formula

1. Lip buzzing.   Start by buzzing your lips without the aid of the mouthpiece or instrument.

2. Middle-register slurring.   Play middle register, mostly scale material, slurred, and with a lyrical tone.

3. Lip-air slurs.   Utilize the harmonic series and play lip-air slurs (no valve or slide changes) starting in the middle register and extending up and down. Also play with other valve and slide combinations.

4. Low register.   Play the lowest register, mostly scale material, slurred; first piano and then forte.

5. Tonguing.   Start with legato tonguing in the middle register, then staccato, and finally double and triple tonguing for advanced players.

6. Upper register.   Play as high as possible, mostly slurred scale- and harmonic-series material. At this point there will be no harm in exploring the outer limits of your ability. Rest briefly after this session.

7. Musical excerpt.   Try out several passages from solos, or from band and orchestra music.

UPPER-REGISTER PERFORMANCE

In recent years the demand has grown for brass players to perform with greater accuracy in the upper register. It is not uncommon to find excellent jazz ensembles and concert bands in junior high schools performing music that was formerly playable by high school and college groups. Still further demands have been made upon high school and college brass players. In many cases such a demand is, perhaps, unreasonable, but the brass players are still held accountable to meet the challenge.

Fear of the Upper Register

Many brass players have been conditioned to fear playing in the upper register. Teachers have told them too often that it is an extremely difficult task to be reserved only for the few "first chair" talents.

Some players never get a chance to play in the upper register. A player on a second or third trumpet or trombone part, for instance, never gets a chance to play in the upper register and gradually loses any confidence to do so.

Breath Control

Correct breath control, previously discussed, is essential for upper-register performance. A greater amount of air pressure than is used for low- and middle-register playing is necessary to achieve and sustain pitches in the upper register. The increase in air pressure is like turning up the water pressure on a garden hose from the water tap.

Tongue Arch

In moving to the upper register, a change in the arch of the tongue helps to produce a more concentrated air stream. Continuing the garden hose analogy, the tongue arch is like channeling the water from the garden hose through a section of hose with a smaller bore. The pressure becomes more concentrated when it passes through the smaller bore hose.

The movement is the same as in whistling from low to high. One cannot whistle a high pitch with a low tongue arch and vice versa. So it is with brass playing; a high tongue arch is needed for high pitches. Some teachers advocate changing the tongue vowel from "ah" to "ee" in moving to the upper register. This concept works, providing that no corresponding smile stretch of the embouchure accompanies the change.

Aids to Upper-Register Performance

Unfortunately, there really are no mechanical aids that make upper-register performance easier. Of course, every music store is well stocked with various devices that claim to do so. There are mouthpieces with extra small throats, small inside cup volume, exaggerated double cups, cushion rims, contour shapes, etc. None of these are satisfactory for all-around performance. Often some seem to aid the upper register in the first few minutes of performance, usually in the music store, but after several hours or days many new problems crop up and a regression takes place. For all-around brass playing a reputable, standard mouthpiece and instrument combination affords the player the greatest variety of range, tone quality, and amplitude.

The problem with high-pitched or small-bore instruments and small mouthpieces is that they allow a player to play in the upper register a little easier, but do not provide the robust tone usually needed in large ensembles. However, some of these devices may be considered for some special solo or chamber-music performance where soft upper-register performance predominates.

MOUTHPIECE PRESSURE

Most brass players use more incoming mouthpiece pressure than they actually need, a habit that usually goes unnoticed until problems with endurance or upper-register performance become manifest. Some mouthpiece pressure is unavoidably needed to form the hermetic seal that prevents air from escaping from the sides of the mouthpiece.

For the trumpet and horn, which use small mouthpieces, the closed-lip aperture for high pitches can be obtained by applying a little extra pressure on the mouthpiece with the lower lip.

ENDURANCE

Endurance is one of the brass player's most persistent problems. The embouchure muscles used in brass performance work very hard holding off the incoming pressure of the mouthpiece as well as manipulating the tension of the lips and the settings of the lip aperture. To meet the rigors of performance, the brass player, like the athlete, must constantly keep his muscles in top condition.

The beginning brass player usually finds a lack of endurance to be the main obstacle inhibiting progress, tiring easily after only minutes of playing because the embouchure muscles have not yet been developed. At this state beginners must be patient enough to put down their instruments and rest when their embouchure muscles become tired. Careful, spaced practice will gradually extend endurance.

Brass players in school ensembles from elementary school through high school should be encouraged to alternate playing with their stand partners. There is rarely a need for all the players to play all the time. For example, in a Sousa march the brass parts are usually written from the beginning of the piece through to the end. However, nothing in the music indicates that each player must play every note in the piece. The brass players will find that if they alternate repeated sections with their stand partners their endurance will be considerably extended.

Even advanced players and professionals have problems with endurance. A great deal of loud upper-register playing will tire even the finest professional brass player. Furthermore, the advanced players who do not play their instruments for a few weeks, or even a few days, will find their endurance noticeably reduced. It may take several weeks for them to regain their former levels of endurance.

In anticipation of particularly strenuous public performances, brass players should begin several weeks in advance to build up their endurance. Also, they must be careful not to overdo any playing session to the point of exhaustion as this will deplete their endurance for days to follow. This is particularly important a day or two before an important performance.

VIBRATO

The use of vibrato on brass instruments, always a matter of some controversy, depends mainly on current fashions and individual taste. Many brass players prefer not to use any vibrato and play with a "straight" or nonemotional tone, whereas others prefer a more emotional, individualized tone that employs some type of vibrato. In certain musical styles—jazz and modern musical theater, for example—the brass instruments are expected to be played consistently with a pronounced vibrato. Most brass-instrument soloists perform with some vibrato at least at times. Since the modern brass player is expected to perform many styles of music in a variety of ensembles, he or she must be able to produce several styles of vibrato as well as the so-called "straight" tone.

All vibrati contain pulsations of intensity with fluctuations of pitch and timbre. The several techniques from which the brass player may choose emphasize either pitch or intensity. Timbre changes automatically with all vibrati.

Emphasis on Pitch

1. Right-hand movement on the trumpet and baritone horn. This technique is accomplished by a slight back-and-forth movement of the player's right hand over the valves which moves the whole instrument back and forth, increasing and decreasing the mouthpiece pressure on the player's lips.

This technique is easy to learn and may be used even with first year students. Also, once developed, it is fairly easy to control and is particularly well-suited for jazz performance. However, many people find it objectionable in concert music because of the wide fluctuations in pitch.

Some highly skilled players use this technique of vibrato, but have learned to narrow the pitch fluctuation so that the vibrato is pleasing for all styles of music. However, few school brass players can develop this level of control and are advised to seek alternate techniques for vibrato, such as the *lip aperture-jaw movement* technique soon to be discussed.

2. Slide movement of the trombone. The player moves the trombone slide back and forth around the slide position. Fine trombonists usually find the position then vibrate the tone by sharpening and neutralizing the pitch. This technique requires a sensitive musician and is usually too subtle for the school trombonist. If it is not controlled well, the alternation of pitch becomes too wide and erratic for most styles of music.

The main disadvantage of using the slide-movement vibrato, perhaps, is that it cannot be used in first position. A break in the continuity of the vibrato then occurs whenever the first position is used. Some professional trombones have a spring device in first position to overcome this problem, but these are rarely found on school instruments. Consequently, this technique is suitable only for a fine trombonist performing with a professional instrument.

3. Right-hand movement in the bell of the horn. A technique for producing a vibrato used by many horn players involves the movement of the player's right hand palm back and forth in the bell. Typically, inexperienced horn players both sharpen and flatten the pitch, but most advanced players who use this technique only sharpen and neutralize the pitch. This technique has several advantages. First, it is relatively easy to control. Second, it does not disturb the delicate horn embouchure. Finally, since a vibrato on the horn is as a matter of fashion only accepted occasionally, the player can add just a little vibrato from time to time without incorporating it into his entire tone production technique. It is, therefore, highly recommended as a vibrato technique for the advanced horn player.

Emphasis on Intensity

1. Lip aperture-jaw movement on all brass instruments. This technique utilizes a slight closing and opening of the player's lip aperture accompanied by an almost imperceptible movement of the jaw. The result is a very slight sharpening and neutralizing of the pitch, but what the listeners perceive is mainly a pulsation of the intensity of the tone.

This technique has many important advantages. First, it can be used by all the brass instruments and is, therefore, relatively easy to teach with mixed groups of brass instruments. Second, since the pitch is altered only slightly, this type of vibrato seems suitable for all styles of music. Third, this technique when used on the trombone allows the trombonist to vibrate uniformly in any position. Fourth, it is the only practical vibrato technique to use on the tuba, since one cannot effectively vibrate this large instrument with the hand movement.

The main disadvantage of the lip aperture-jaw movement vibrato is that it takes a great deal of practice to bring it under control. Another disadvantage cited by horn players is that it uses too much embouchure movement and thus adds to the risk of accidentally shifting to another tone in the harmonic series.

The lip aperture-jaw movement vibrato is utilized successfully by many prominent brass performers and is highly recommended for the student.

2. Pulsation of the air column on all brass instruments. This type of vibrato is produced by a pulsation of the player's whole breathing system very similar to laughter. It is a style that has been especially fashionable with French brass players. The technique is difficult to acquire, and once it is incorporated into the player's tone production it is difficult to eliminate or modify. However, the main objection to the pulsating air-column vibrato is the "nanny-goat" sound which has very limited appeal to audiences and is not well-suited to most musical styles.

Speed of Vibrato

The speed of the vibrato, that is, the rate of fluctuations, is usually determined by the emotional quality of the music. However, the speed of between five and seven fluctuations per second seems to please most listeners.

When to Begin Vibrato Development

Brass teachers usually delay introducing the vibrato until their students have gained a strong command of their instrument, typically after several years of study. This approach seems logical for a highly motivated student taking individual lessons, but for average school brass players such a delay seems to inhibit their progress. With vibrato the young brass players suddenly sound more like the fine brass players they use for models and their satisfaction with their own performance increases dramatically. Consequently, it seems to be desirable to introduce the vibrato as soon as any beginning brass player can sustain a steady tone, probably after a few months of study.

TONGUING AND ARTICULATION

Articulation in brass-instrument performance serves the same basic functions as in speech, namely, to make the sounds more distinct and also more expressive. The beginning brass-instrument student is often under the misconception that there are only two styles of articulation: smooth (legato) and detached (staccato). In fact, there are many styles, which will be discussed here.

Tongue Placement

Before releasing the air at the start of the articulation, the player generally places the tongue in the same position that one uses to pronounce "*doo*" or "*too.*" Each player may place his tongue in a slightly different position, but the *doo* or *too* pronouncement is a useful starting point for the player to explore his individual tongue placement. Almost all varieties of tongue placement are acceptable *if* they produce the effect the player desires. The "spitting the seed from the tip of the tongue" method of tonguing where the tongue protrudes between the teeth should be avoided, however, since it interferes with the proper vibration of the lips and produces an articulation that sounds too explosive.

Tonguing Styles

The choice of tonguing used for articulation is at the discretion of the player. He must interpret the markings in the score according to the style of the composition, similar to the string player's decisions on bowing. The printed score is usually extremely vague with regard to the actual tonguing a player should use. For instance, the marking ⌒♪♪♪ simply indicates that the notes under the phrase mark or slur should be played legato or phrased together but does not necessarily indicate the method of tonguing to be used. In the above case, the player may decide to slur each note if the notes are different pitches, or use a legato tonguing on each note, or slur some notes and legato-tongue the others.

A further complication results from the fact that a great deal of music appears without any expression or phrasing marks. Unmarked music is not necessarily played detached. Players must be able to recognize the musical styles in order to choose suitable tonguings.

Legato Tonguing

Legato tonguing should be used exclusively by beginning players as it is the method of tonguing that least disturbs the air stream and lip vibrations and is also the easiest to control. The player gently articulates a silent *doo* on the trumpet and horn and a *daw* on the trombone, baritone and tuba. If desired, still smoother articulations can be achieved with the use of *thoo* or *thaw*.

Usually, musical passages played by the entire brass section can be made to sound more articulate when a legato tonguing is substituted for written slurs. A pure slur across a valve change unavoidably results in a slight blurring between tones. However, the use of legato tonguing allows the player to change valve combinations with more clarity.

The trombonist, of course, must substitute legato tonguing for most slurs in order to avoid the glissando that occurs between most slide positions. There are exceptions, however, when the music calls for the special effect of slurring across harmonics.

Staccato Tonguing

Staccato tonguing is more difficult to execute on brass instruments than legato tonguing because the tones must be separated and stopped with the breath. *Staccato* is one of those vague musical terms meaning *detached.* How short the tone and how much separation between tones is subject to a wide variety of interpretations.

Stopping the tone of a brass instrument is usually accomplished with the breathing muscles. Only in very rare circumstances should the tone be stopped with the tongue by articulating *toot* or *doot.* This effect is too abrupt in most cases, but is occasionally required in jazz performance.

All other staccato tones should be stopped with the breathing muscles, similar to articulating *too* or *taw.* The tone when stopped with the breathing muscles has a ringing quality to it similar to a string pizzicato or a xylophone tone.

Theoretically, the staccato marking ♩̇ refers to the duration of the tone and not necessarily to its attack. However, in rapid staccato passages, the start or tongue attack is usually made more pointed or definite.

Extreme staccatissimo should rarely be used in brass-instrument performance because it produces a harsh tone. Even the more common staccato could be considered a special effect that should be used sparingly.

Accent Tonguing

Bell-like, accent tonguings are uniquely exciting when played on brass instruments. The typical brass fanfare utilizes this type of tonguing almost exclusively.

Accent tonguing is not difficult to produce. It requires an ample supply of air and a quick release of the tongue. The tones should not be poked, since the focus of the action should be on the release of the air and not the tongue movement.

Sforzando Tonguing

The sforzando is another special effect used mainly in jazz-ensemble performance. It is similar to accent tonguing, but more exaggerated. Many players find they need to place the tongue between the teeth in sort of a spitting action in order to achieve the desired effect. The result is an explosive, heavy attack.

Double and Triple Tonguing

Advanced brass players have some special techniques for tonguing passages of music that are too fast to be played with single strokes of the tongue: they are, *double* and *triple* tonguing. Simply stated, the player can produce additional articulations with the back of his tongue while the front is recoiling for its next attack. The back of the tongue action is similar to silently pronouncing *goo* or *gaw*.

The only difference between double and triple tonguing is the alternation pattern. Double tonguing is used mainly in duple passages and employs a pattern similar to *doo-goo-doo-goo-doo*, etc. Triple tonguing is most convenient for groups of triplets and uses a pattern similar to *doo-doo-goo-doo-doo-goo-doo*, etc.

These patterns may seem like tongue twisters at first, but most people should have no trouble with the pattern, *kitty-kitty-kitty,* etc., which is very similar to double tonguing. Nevertheless, the development of well controlled double and triple tonguing on a brass instrument usually requires a great deal of patient practice over months or even years.

It is beyond the scope of a college brass-methods course to expect the development of either double- or triple-tonguing skills, but instrumental music teachers must know how to develop these skills with their advanced brass-instrument performers.

INSTRUMENTS

Trumpet/Cornet

The traditional distinctions between the trumpet and cornet have nearly disappeared. The trumpet still has slightly more cylindrical tubing than the cornet, and until recently there was a definite difference in the tone quality and performance characteristics of the two instruments. The trumpet had the more strident tone and the cornet was more flexible in performing fast, running passages. However, modern instruments can be played in any manner the player desires. Both the trumpet and cornet can be played to sound brilliant or mellow with equal flexibility. Today, the trumpet is the more popular instrument, probably owing to its prominence in jazz and popular music.

Trumpet/Cornet intonations.   There are two main areas that are noticeably out of tune even with the best instruments: (1) the fifth harmonic (fourth overtone), and (2) valve combinations 1-3 and 1-2-3.

1. The fifth harmonic of the harmonic series is acoustically flat for traditional Western music intonation. Since the harmonic is flat (about 0.14 of a semitone) all the valve combinations added to that harmonic will also be flat. The following notes are the most troublesome:

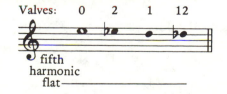

All of these tones are flat and need to be corrected. The most practical solution on the trumpet and cornet is for the player to raise slightly each of the pitches with his embouchure. It is relatively easy to "lip" up 0.14 of a semitone. The important thing is that the player should expect these tones to be flat and be ready to correct them when needed.

2. *Valve combinations 1-3 and 1-2-3 are extremely sharp.* The reasons for their sharpness are complicated, but suffice it to say that manufacturers build their trumpets and cornets to play best in tune with single valves engaged and next best with the most used combinations. Since the combinations 1-3 and 1-2-3 are the least used they contain the most intonation problems.

All valve combinations are out of tune. For instance, the valve combination 1-2 is sharp approximately 0.12 of a semitone. The combination 2-3 is also sharp about 0.16 of a semitone. These are corrected with a slight "lipping" down by the player.

The combination 1-3 is sharp about 0.32 of a semitone and the combination 1-2-3 is still sharper—about 0.55 (approximately a quarter tone sharp). Fortunately, these combinations are only encountered at the lower end of the range and only occasionally present problems:

Third-valve extension. To compensate for these out-of-tune valve combinations, most trumpets and cornets are provided with a third-valve ring and extension slide. The player uses the ring to extend the third-valve slide out, lowering the pitch.

Horn

Single F horn. The single horn pitched in F is the horn most commonly used in the public schools. It has a full, warm tone suitable for all instrumental ensembles. Its main problem is that the harmonics in the middle and upper register (harmonics six through sixteen) are so close together that the player usually has difficulty locating the correct one.

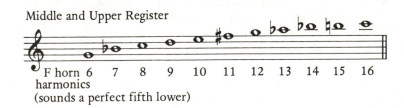

Single B♭ horn. The single B♭ horn has a shorter length than the single F horn—about nine feet compared with the F horn's twelve. Its harmonic series is pitched a perfect fourth higher, resulting in wider-spaced harmonics in its middle and upper register.

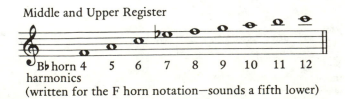

The Bb horn is lighter and plays more easily in its upper register than the F horn. Its big problem is its tone quality in the middle and lower registers. The tone quality here is smaller than with the F horn, and many players in large ensembles find they must work too hard in order to be heard.

Double F-Bb horn.   The best of both horns is combined in the double horn. It is really two instruments in one, with two sets of slides, one for the F section and another for the Bb. A thumb valve enables the player to switch between the two. The player can use the more comfortable upper register of the Bb section and then switch back to the F section for the warmer tones of the F section in the middle and low registers.

The player must decide when he should shift between the F and Bb sections of the horn. Although some differences of opinion exist, the following chart is a convenient general guide:

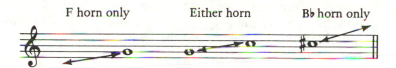

Which horn for school use?   Beginning horn players should start with the single F horn for its better over-all tone quality, its lower cost and lighter weight. The single Bb horn, though fine in its upper register, has a small tone quality in its most commonly used middle register.

Advanced players should use the double F-Bb horn when their music calls for upper-register as well as middle-register playing. If the school can provide these instruments, players on first and third horn parts should use them.

Many directors find that the horns used for concert performance are too delicate to use while marching. When possible, the school should provide alternate instruments for marching bands. These include the *altonium, alto horn* or *melophonium.*

Horn intonation problems and solutions.   The horns have the same basic intonation problems as all the valved brass instruments: the flat fifth harmonic and sharp valve combinations. However, the hornist has a quick solution for these problems. The player can compensate for flatness by opening the cupped right hand slightly in the bell, and for sharpness by cupping the hand further into the bell.

The flat fifth harmonic notes for the F horn are:

Trombone

Single tenor trombone.   The trombone most often used in the schools is the single tenor trombone. Its harmonic series is one octave below the trumpet starting on Bb. It is non-transposing and is read mainly in the bass clef.

Compared with comparable woodwinds and string instruments, well-made single tenor trombones are relatively inexpensive. They are manufactured with a number of bore sizes— from 0.491 inches (small) to 0.542 inches (large)—and bell sizes—from 7 inches (small) to 10 inches (large). A single tenor trombone with medium bore and bell size is usually recommended for the beginning trombone student.

Single bass trombone. The single bass trombone is actually only a large-bore tenor trombone. It has the same harmonic series and range as the tenor trombone but produces a slightly darker tone quality. Bass-trombone bore sizes generally range from about 0.542 inches to 0.565 inches.

Double bass trombone with F attachment. The single bass trombone is less common than the bass trombone (large-bore size) with an F attachment. Both instruments are well suited for third trombone parts in both the band and the orchestra.

Tenor and bass trombone with F attachment. The favorite instrument of advanced and professional trombonists is the tenor or bass trombone with an F attachment. The F attachment is an additional set of tubing activated by a thumb trigger and rotary valve that changes the basic harmonic series from B♭ to F a perfect fourth lower.
 The F attachment adds versatility to the trombone. For one thing, it eases the problem of moving the slide great distances. Simply by pressing the trigger the player makes an additional set of tones available. For example, the following passage can be played entirely with the first position, second position, and thumb trigger:

The following chart further illustrates some of the basic notes playable with only first and second positions on the B♭ and F sections of the trombone:

In addition to simplifying slide-position movement, the F attachment also adds a perfect 4th to the bottom range of the trombone as follows:

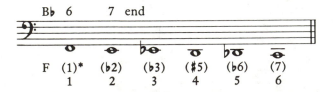

The trombone using the F attachment has only six slide positions rather than the seven on the B♭ section. The reason for this is that the F attachment adds about four feet of tubing to the basic B♭ instrument, without changing the bell and slide. Consequently, in order to obtain seven full positions it would necessitate a slide several inches longer. However, six positions are made possible by a spring that extends the first position slightly and extends the slide for sixth position slightly beyond the usual seventh position of the B♭ section.

*Compared with B♭ positions.

130

The following chart shows an approximate comparison of the seven slide positions on the regular B♭ section with the six slide positions on the F attachment:

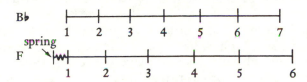

Baritone Horn

In Europe this instrument is generally called a *euphonium.* Years ago there was an actual difference between the baritone horn and the euphonium in that the euphonium had larger bore tubing. The relationship was similar to that of the tenor and bass trombone, but for all practical purposes modern instrument manufacturers have eliminated these differences.

Baritone-horn intonation problems and solutions.   The baritone horn has the same basic intonational problems as all the valved brass instruments: the flat fifth harmonic and sharp valve combinations.

The fifth harmonic is about 0.14 of a semitone flat. This can most easily be corrected by the player "lipping" up.

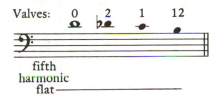

Fourth valve.   Most baritone horns are built with a fourth valve to help compensate for the extreme sharpness of the valve combinations 1-3 and 1-2-3. The fourth valve adds a perfect 4th of tubing to the basic instrument, similar to the F attachment on the trombone. To compensate for sharpness, the player substitutes the fourth valve for the valve combinations 1-3, and the fourth and second valves (2-4) for the extremely sharp valve combinations 1-2-3. This greatly improves the intonation of these troublesome valve combinations.

The fourth valve also has the advantage of adding a perfect 4th to the bottom range of the baritone horn. This allows the baritone horn to play down into the tuba range.

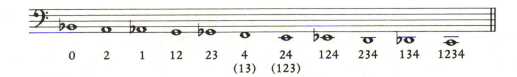

131

Tuba

BB♭ upright-bell tuba.   The BB♭ upright-bell tuba is the tuba most preferred by school ensemble directors. Its bell points toward the ceiling and thus avoids the overpowering direct-ness of the bell-front tuba.

BB♭ upright-bell tubas are made in a variety of shapes and weights. The lighter ones are designed mainly for young players and have a somewhat smaller tone quality. The heavier ones have larger bore sizes and should be used by all advanced players. The larger-bore instru-ments have solid low registers and blend well with other instruments.

Most of the BB♭ upright-bell tubas are equipped with a fourth valve (to be discussed sub-sequently) making them extremely versatile for all styles of tuba performance.

BB♭ bell-front tuba.   This instrument is essentially the same as the BB♭ upright-bell tuba, but has its bell pointing forward. The BB♭ bell-front tuba was often known as a *recording* model. This designation goes back to the early days of phonograph recording when the forward angle of the tuba bell enabled sound engineers to obtain a better tuba sound than with the upright bell. Today, however, owing to the new techniques the forward position of the tuba bell is not required for recording.

Played by a fine performer, the bell-front tuba makes a fine solo instrument. But in the hands of an insensitive player it can easily overpower any ensemble. The instrument usually is made with a fourth valve like the BB♭ upright-bell tuba.

E♭ upright-bell tuba.   The E♭ upright-bell tuba is a smaller, higher-pitched version of the BB♭ upright-bell tuba. It once was a very popular school instrument. It has lost its popularity because instrument makers have produced superior BB♭ upright-bell tubas just as light as the E♭, but with better tone quality and the added lower range.

BB♭ sousaphone.   The BB♭ sousaphone is the marching-band tuba most widely used in the schools. It was designed for marching and not for concert performance. However, since marching bands are so popular, many schools that cannot afford to purchase both sets of instruments end up with only BB♭ sousaphones and are forced to use the marching sousa-phones in place of concert tubas.

The sousaphone is a poor concert instrument for several reasons. First, it has its bell pointed front with all the disadvantages of the bell-front tuba. With four to six bell-front sousaphones playing in a moderately sized band, for instance, the balance is impossible to control.

Second, the tone quality of even the best sousaphone is almost without exception inferior to a comparable BB♭ upright-bell tuba. Modern sousaphones are usually made from some sort of fiberglas material to make them lighter to carry, and fiberglas cannot compete with brass as a fine quality resonating material.

Third, sousaphones are rarely made with a fourth valve. Consequently, the intonation in the lower register is always extremely poor for concert performance.

E♭ sousaphone.   The E♭ sousaphone is a smaller version of the BB♭ sousaphone. At one time it was a popular instrument in the schools, providing a marching instrument for players who had started on the E♭ tuba. It was also used to allow trumpet and horn players to transfer to the E♭ sousaphone with a minimum of retraining. This transfer was not too dif-ficult because of a trick in reading clefs. The trumpet or horn player can read the F clef as though it were the G clef but containing three additional flats. For example:

The example above shows that the basic key signature with three flats for the F clef equals a key signature of no sharps or flats for the G clef.

The disadvantages of the E♭ sousaphone are many. Because it is pitched a fourth higher it has fewer lower tones than the BB♭ instruments. Also, E♭ sousaphones are made only with three valves and are, therefore, subject to intonational difficulties in the lower register. These drawbacks, combined with the bell front, make the E♭ sousaphone an extremely poor concert instrument and only a fair one for marching.

CC upright-bell tuba. This instrument is rarely found in the schools, but is a favorite of professional orchestra players. It generally has a somewhat more concentrated tone than the BB♭ upright-bell tuba. Its overtone series on C fundamental makes it easier to finger and play in tune in the orchestral keys than the BB♭ tuba. A school with a fine orchestral program should, if budget allows, consider the purchase of one CC upright-bell tuba.

Fourth valve. Most quality-made tubas contain a fourth valve which, as with the baritone horn, is used to compensate for the extreme sharpness of valve combinations 1-3 (+ 0.32), and 1-2-3 (+ 0.55), as shown for the BB♭ tuba on the following chart:

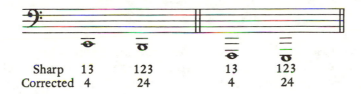

	Sharp	13	123	13	123
	Corrected	4	24	4	24

The fourth valve also extends the bottom range as follows for the BB♭ tuba:

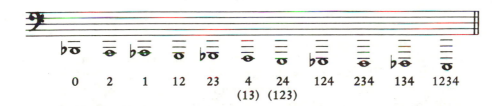

0   2   1   12   23   4   24   124   234   134   1234
                    (13) (123)

UNUSUAL BRASS INSTRUMENTS

There are several other brass instruments that are used occasionally in the schools. They are used mostly for special purposes.

B♭ Flügelhorn

This instrument grew out of the Saxhorn family, of which the present-day cornet and baritone horns were also members. It is pitched in B♭ like the cornet and trumpet, but its bore shape is almost entirely conical. It uses a slightly deeper mouthpiece and has a larger bell than the cornet or trumpet. With these characteristics the resulting tone is large, full, and mellow. It plays very well in the alto register of the instrument.

The B♭ flügelhorn can be used in several interesting ways. It makes an excellent substitute for cornet or trumpet on third cornet parts in the band or wind ensemble. Since the original parts call for playing mostly in the alto register, or the lower end of the cornet or trumpet register, the B♭ flügelhorn takes over these parts with greater ease than either the cornet or trumpet. Also, the mellow tone quality of the flügelhorn makes a perfect intermediary instrument between the trumpet or cornet and the horn.

The flügelhorn can be used in the jazz ensemble as a solo instrument, or as a substitute for the horn. It adds an interesting color to the ensemble.

F Melophonium

Looking like an oversized trumpet, with its bell pointing forward, this relatively new instrument is fast gaining popularity. Its harmonic series is pitched in F, but since it starts an octave above the horn, traditional trumpet fingering may be used. A trumpet or treble-clef baritone-horn player adapts to this instrument immediately, and a horn player needs only a little more time to become accustomed to it.

The melophonium makes an excellent substitute for the horn in the marching band. It can be played comfortably while marching and its bell front and general tone quality is considerably better suited to the marching band than the horn.

A number of famous jazz ensembles have added this instrument to their brass sections in recent years. Its bell front records better than the horn and its tone blends extremely well as an alto voice between soprano trumpets and tenor and bass trombones.

E♭-F Altonium

The altonium was designed as a substitute instrument for the horn in the marching band. It is pitched in E♭, but has a special crook to change its overtone series to F. Like the melophonium its F overtone series is pitched an octave higher than the horn and requires trumpet fingering rather than horn fingering. This allows either a trumpet or horn player to make the switch to the altonium easily.

The altonium is shaped like a small baritone horn and is extremely comfortable to carry while marching. Its tone quality, however, is not as interesting as the melophonium or horn and, therefore, the altonium is rarely used outside of the marching band.

Trombonium

The trombonium is pitched and shaped like the baritone horn, but with more cylindrical tubing and a smaller bell. Its tone quality resembles the trombone. With its three piston valves it is actually a reshaped valve trombone. The trombonium was designed for use in marching bands as a substitute for the slide trombone. Its shape and valves make it more convenient to march with than the trombone, but its tone quality is usually inferior.

MOUTHPIECES

There are many variables in the manufacture of brass-instrument mouthpieces. The following discussion may be useful in aiding students to find the right combination of variables to enable them to perform to their maximum potential.

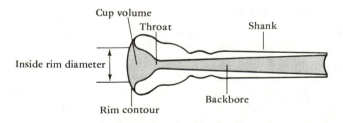

Figure 27. Brass-mouthpiece variables.

134

Inside Rim Diameter

A mouthpiece with a relatively wide inside rim diameter usually aids a player to obtain a full tone quality and wider range. For the trumpet and horn a mouthpiece with a wide inside rim diameter enables the player's lips to move freely in controling the lip aperture. An inside rim diameter that is too small inhibits lip movement and encourages the player to use excess pressure to close the lip aperture.

If the inside rim diameter is too large, however, the tone will lack focus and the player's embouchure muscles will fatigue easily from overuse.

Cup Volume

The cup volume, which includes the depth of the mouthpiece cup, mainly affects the quality of tone: the greater the volume or deeper the cup, the darker and fuller the tone. Conversely, the smaller the cup volume or the shallower the cup, the brighter and smaller the tone produced will be.

The loudness of the tone is also affected by the cup volume. It is easier to play loudly with a mouthpiece that has a large cup volume than with one that has a smaller cup volume. In general, a mouthpiece with a large cup volume is suitable for the louder playing usually required for marching bands and jazz ensembles, but for lighter performance, such as solo and chamber-music ensemble, a smaller cup volume is better.

Throat

The throat is the hole drilled through the center of the mouthpiece cup. Since it is the narrowest gap in the mouthpiece-instrument combination, its dimensions are very important. In general, a mouthpiece with a narrow throat will offer a great deal of resistance to the player and make loud playing more difficult than soft playing. If the throat is very large, the lack of resistance will make soft playing more difficult than loud playing.

The dimensions of the throat should match the type of performance required. For a marching band or a jazz ensemble, a more open throat will usually be better than a closed throat. For light solo and chamber-music ensemble playing, a mouthpiece with a small throat will usually aid the player in controling softer musical passages. However, a medium open throat will usually satisfy the widest diversity of performance needs.

The throat is one dimension that can be changed easily. It can be enlarged by carefully drilling the throat with the next larger size drill bit. Obviously, once enlarged the throat cannot be closed again.

Rim Contour

The rim contour is the roundness or flatness of the rim. Choosing a shape is mainly a matter of comfort and accommodation of the player's tooth formation and does not seem to affect the sound. A player with ragged front teeth who uses a great deal of pressure will find a flatter shaped rim more comfortable than a rounded rim. Some special mouthpieces are made with an extra wide, flat rim for this purpose.

A curved rim with a fairly sharp inner rim bite will afford the player the maximum of control. Most symphony brass players prefer this latter combination, while many jazz players prefer the flatter rim. All players should aim toward playing with less and less pressure on a rounder, sharper-edged rim. Resorting to a wide, flat rim usually indicates that the player is using too much mouthpiece pressure; the cure is less pressure rather than a more comfortable rim.

Shank

The shank is the part of the mouthpiece that extends into the mouthpiece receiver on the instrument. If the taper of the mouthpiece shank is too narrow it will allow the mouthpiece to extend too far into the instrument's leadpipe. This will cause some sharpness because it shortens the instrument, and it may also contribute to the production of an unclear tone quality. The mouthpiece must not butt against the start of the leadpipe.

If the shank is too short, or its taper too wide, it will not allow the mouthpiece to move far enough into the mouthpiece receiver. This may cause flattening and also an unclear tone quality.

To correct these problems, the player should experiment with different lengths of shanks while keeping the other dimensions of the mouthpiece constant. If problems persist the player should consult a reputable mouthpiece and instrument repairman.

Backbore

The backbore is the inside conical flare of the shank end of the mouthpiece. In general, a backbore that has been drilled with a narrow flare creates more air resistance and makes louder playing more difficult than a backbore with a wider flare. A backbore flare that is too open causes the tone to spread, lacking a vibrant core. It also seems to hinder upper-register playing. Ease of performance in the upper register seems to be aided by the use of a straighter, less flared backbore.

BASIC CARE AND MAINTENANCE

Fortunately, brass instruments are relatively rugged and require only simple maintenance and a moderate amount of care. It is well worth the time to instruct students on the proper assemblage, care, and maintenance of their instruments. This will avoid many problems in the future.

Dents

Dents are the most common damage inflicted upon brass instruments by students. In varying degrees, all dents affect the resonating quality of the tone and the intonation, especially if they occur in the mouthpiece leadpipe and tuning slides.

Denting can be avoided with care. Students should never leave their instruments on their chairs, stands, or on the floor. Many dents are incurred by students knocking instruments off chairs and stands while moving through an ensemble set up. The safest place for an instrument is in its padded case.

Instruments can also get dented in their cases. Loose mouthpieces, oil bottles, etc. can shift around while being carried and cause denting. Fixing dents is expensive and puts the instrument out of commission while it is at the repair shop. By contrast, preventative care is simple.

Stuck Mouthpieces

After dents, the next most common repair problem for young brass players is probably stuck mouthpieces. Of course, mouthpieces don't just get stuck through normal use. Usually, the instrument has been dropped or bumped on the mouthpiece end. Occasionally, a student will put the mouthpiece on the instrument and give it a healthy tap to make sure it stays on. It will!

There is a very simple device called a *mouthpiece puller,* a type of special vise, that pulls out stuck mouthpieces without damage to either the mouthpiece or instrument. In no case should pliers or a hammer be used to unstick a mouthpiece as the brass is too soft for either.

Stuck Slides

Tuning slides and valve slides often get stuck on brass instruments. They usually can be removed by inserting a rag approximately two feet long through the "U" of the slide, then twisting it half way through to form sort of a pull rope. Several short snappy tugs on the rag should set the slide free. If not, it is best turned over to an instrument repairman.

Why Cleaning?

It is amazing what ends up inside of brass instruments, especially during football or basketball games: chewing gum, colas, etc. All contain sugar that hardens inside the tubing and valves of the instrument, causing valves and slides to stick and gradually deadening the tone quality. If at all possible, sweets should be avoided before brass playing. More realistically, the brass player should know that the instrument must be periodically cleaned.

Bathing. Every few weeks the brass player should plan on a complete cleaning of the instrument, including bathing it. The instrument should be flushed through with a hose using medium warm water (never hot water, which will melt the lacquer). A little dishwashing liquid detergent should be poured into the bell in the process.

Cleaning. After flushing, the entire instrument, except for the rotary valves, should be disassembled. Each slide and tube should then be cleaned with a special brass-instrument *snake brush*. Valves should then be wiped with a lint-free cloth and valve casings swabbed with a special swab tool. Each part should then be lubricated and the instrument reassembled.

Lubricating valve slides and tuning slides. Special slide grease is available at music stores for lubricating the slides. For bulk use an equal and less expensive substitute is *Lanolin Anydrous*, available in jars under that name at drug stores. In emergencies petroleum jelly can be used. Slides should be lubricated after cleaning and before instruments are stored for any length of time.

Lubricating valve caps. The threads on the upper and lower valve caps should receive a little dab of the grease that is used on the slides.

Lubricating piston valves. Only a commercial valve oil should be used for lubricating valves. It is made with the right balance of ingredients to keep the delicate valves working. The player must be careful, however, not to mix brands of oil which may not be compatible. Some brands contain a *silicone* additive which will not mix with oils made without the silicone.

Oiling between cleaning is best done through the holes in the bottom of the valve casings. There is no need to take out the valves to oil them except during a complete cleaning.

Lubricating rotary valves. The rotary valve used on the horn, some tubas and baritone horns, and the F attachment of the trombone require oil occasionally. Some manufacturers claim that oil is needed only about every month or two. Rotary valves should not be dismantled by students. The valve can be oiled without even removing the string. First, the bottom valve cap should be removed exposing the back head bearing. A drop or two of commercial rotary-valve oil should then be placed on the back head bearing. Finally, the valve cap should be replaced.

Lubricating trombone slides. The main slide on the trombone needs a special extra-lightweight oil. Commercial trombone slide oil is the simplest for young players to use. However, many professionals and advanced players prefer to put a very thin glaze of cold cream on the main slide with plain water thinly sprayed over the cold cream. The cold cream holds the water in tiny beads and is extremely effective. Plastic spray bottles, discarded from all sorts of commercial products, can be used to hold the water. The cold cream and water lubrication takes a little more care, but is superior to oil.

Care of Outside Finishes

Brass players prefer their instruments with a variety of outside finishes, such as clear lacquer, silver or gold plating, and even polished brass.

Clear-lacquer finish. The clear-lacquer finish is the most popular finish for brass instruments, producing a brilliant gold appearance that is very attractive. The finish is accomplished by highly polishing the natural brass and then coating it with a thin clear lacquer that is similar to clear nail polish. Very hot water or heat can melt it. Skin and sugar acids eat away at it and sharp objects can scrape it off. Therefore, this finish takes a great deal of special care.

The whole instrument should be wiped clean with a soft jeweler's cloth before it is put back into its case. A clear paste wax, such as the type used for cars, should be applied monthly to the finish to help prolong its life.

Silver-plated finish. Silver plating is a more costly finishing process than clear lacquer, but is probably less expensive in the long run because of its durability. Many manufacturers claim that silver plating improves the tone quality of the instrument, whereas clear lacquer dulls it somewhat.

The silver finish is easy to care for. The instrument should be completely wiped free of marks with a soft jeweler's cloth before it is put away. A tarnish-preventing silver polish should be periodically applied when tarnish appears. When properly applied and cared for, a silver-plated finish can last ten to twenty years and makes an excellent finish for school instruments.

Gold-plated finish. Gold plating is much too costly for all players except perhaps a few professionals. Most players who have used a gold-plated instrument claim it provides the best finish available. Other players, however, have not found it to be superior to the silver-plated finish.

Polished brass. A few players prefer only a polished brass finish for their brass instruments, claiming that the natural brass has more ring than any lacquer or plated finish. Unfinished brass must be constantly polished to keep the instrument from looking like bathroom plumbing, however. Since it tarnishes in only a day or two after being polished, it is not a very practical finish for brass instruments.

Chapter 6
TEACHING BRASS INSTRUMENTS IN THE SCHOOLS

PHILOSOPHY

The general philosophy for the instrumental program in the schools is that it exists for the students' musical growth in skills and understanding. Bands, orchestras, and chamber-music ensembles are vehicles through which a student experiences and discovers music.

GRADE LEVEL FOR BEGINNERS

The appropriate grade level for beginning brass players is an important decision in the development of a solid instrumental curriculum. The decision usually becomes a compromise between two factors: the optimum readiness age and the optimum social age.

The optimum readiness age at which brass players seem to progress more rapidly, according to recent studies, is the *seventh* grade.[1] The problem is that by the seventh grade, a student is usually committed to many social organizations, such as Girl Scouts, Boy Scouts, intramural sports, swim teams, tennis lessons, religious clubs, etc. These take away time from instrumental music studies. Therefore, while the seventh grade would appear to have some advantage in readiness, it is usually too late for students to commit themselves to studying a brass instrument wholeheartedly.

Many successful instrumental music programs start their beginners in grades *four* or *five*. At this level progress is moderate, but commitment avid. Offering instrumental music study from grades four or five, though the student's performing skill may progress slowly, affords an excellent opportunity for expanding the traditional role of performing groups to include many interesting musical activities. An example of this approach can be found in Brent Heisinger's *Comprehensive Musicianship Through Band Performance.* In his preface, Heisinger notes that his curriculum is designed so that:

(1) musical understanding evolves from *actual performance.*

(2) selected activities ensure the systematic introduction of a number of concepts, and

(3) students are placed in varied musicianly roles—performing (small and large ensembles), improvising, composing, transcribing, arranging, conducting, rehearsing, and analyzing (visually and aurally).[2]

---

[1]George Duerksen, *Teaching Instrumental Music* (Washington, D. C.: Music Educators National Conference, 1972), pp. 8, 9.

[2]Brent Heisinger, *Comprehensive Musicianship Through Band Performance* (Menlo Park, Cal.: Addison-Wesley Publishing Co., 1973).

Tests

There is no foolproof method of predicting success for instrumental students.[3] There are, of course, many tests in use in the schools, including standardized tests designed to measure such qualities as *aptitude, musicality, musical intelligence, talent, achievement*, etc.

Instrumental music instructors also use non-standardized tests and other criteria to "identify" talent and "predict" success with instruments, such as school tests, school grades, teachers' ratings, and even finger-dexterity tests. However, the single factor with the highest correlation with success in instrumental music is the student's *desire to play the instrument.*[4]

Announcements

All students and their parents should be adequately notified that the school is offering beginning brass-instrument instruction. This should be done the semester prior to the start of instruction. Each student should be given at least two hand-outs fully explaining the program along with sign-up sheets to be signed by the parents and returned. The instructor should be sure to include a phone number on the hand-outs so he can be reached to answer questions from parents.

Demonstrations

Perhaps, the most effective recruitment tool is the live demonstration given before small groups of prospective students. The program should include a small chamber-music ensemble and a short solo on each instrument and can be performed by upper classmen of the same school district. Students should be allowed to ask questions and, perhaps, even to try to play a tone or two.

The demonstration should be kept short and informal. At the end of the demonstration the instructor should take the name of each student who expresses an interest in one of the instruments.

Follow Up

As soon as possible after the demonstration the instructor should meet with each student who expressed a desire to play a brass instrument and explain the amount of hard work and daily practice involved. The parents of each of these students should be contacted by mail or by phone. A written contract of commitment should be signed by both parents and students. All persons involved should have full knowledge of what is expected from them, i.e., instrument procurement, daily practice at home, rehearsal schedules, etc.

Selecting the Right Instrument

The desire to play a particular instrument has previously been cited as, perhaps, the best predictor for success. Therefore, students should be allowed to study the instrument of their choice. This can, however, create some problems since not all students will be entirely suited to the instruments they have chosen.

For instance, many beginning students find the small mouthpiece of the trumpet to be uncomfortable. After a few weeks of performance they may experience difficulties playing in the trumpet's upper register. Others find endurance on the trumpet a major problem in-

[3]George Duerksen, *Teaching Instrumental Music* (Washington, D. C.: Music Educators National Conference, 1972), pp. 6, 7.

[4]*Ibid*, p. 7.

hibiting their progress. These students might adjust more easily to the trombone, baritone horn, and tuba with their larger mouthpieces.

Some beginning horn students have a great deal of difficulty finding the correct tones because of the closeness of the tones of the harmonic series in the horn's middle and upper registers. Keen pitch discrimination is especially needed for horn playing.

The mouthpieces and performing ranges of the trombone and the baritone horn seem to create the least problems for beginning brass players. Consequently, beginners who find the trumpet or horn mouthpiece too small or the tuba mouthpiece too large should be encouraged to explore the trombone or the baritone horn instead.

Every beginner's trombone should be equipped with a counterweight on the main tuning slide to aid the young student in holding the instrument more comfortably. Occasionally, grade-school children have difficulty stretching out to seventh position on the trombone. However, this should not prevent them from studying the trombone since seventh position is only rarely used at the beginning level. Furthermore, the problem can be eliminated by installing a special extension handle on the slide grip.

The great size of the tuba often causes adjustment problems for some young players. A tuba stand aids some students, but others will not be able to cope with the instrument.

Switching Instruments

Since most of the basic suitability problems that students encounter only become apparent after a few weeks of study, school instrumental-music instructors need to set aside time in their schedules to help students switch instruments when the need becomes obvious. A trumpet student, for instance, who after a few weeks of study still has a great deal of difficulty playing above (written) third-space c, may enjoy more success on a trombone or a baritone horn. Or, occasionally, there is a trombone player with an unusually bright tone quality and effortless upper register and a poor lower register. This player is probably better suited for the trumpet and should be allowed to experiment briefly with the new instrument. There are countless stories of great performers who had a poor time of it in music until they found the instrument that was to be theirs for life.

SCHEDULING BEGINNING BRASS CLASSES

Class Size

Class sizes from eight to twelve have been found to be excellent for beginning instrument study. Too large a class reduces individual attention and slows the progress of the group, whereas too small a class generally becomes an inefficient utilization of a teacher's time.

Class Formats

Possible formats for beginning brass class are listed below in order of desirability from most to least:[5]

1. Two thirty-minute homogeneous classes per week. This format is used by many successful instrumental-music programs. It affords the students a great opportunity for progress. Meeting students twice a week allows the instructor a chance to correct faulty playing techniques and to reenforce correct techniques. Since students cannot always be counted on to practice consistently at home, playing twice a week under the supervision of the instructor assures regularly spaced performance. The thirty-minute time block for each class seems to

---

[5]For a more detailed discussion of scheduling music classes consult: Robert H. Klotman, *Scheduling Music Classes* (Washington, D. C.: Music Educators National Conference, 1968).

be well suited for maintaining the attention and endurance of young players. By using the homogeneous class (all trumpets, all horns, etc.) the instructor can deal with common problems while maintaining a high level of student interest.

2. One thirty-minute homogeneous class per week. This format is less than ideal, but it still affords the beginning brass student a chance for moderate progress. Its main drawback is that the instructor only supervises the student's playing once a week, leaving the rest of the week for the development of poor playing techniques. Students who do not practice at home will make very little progress in this format. The instructor needs to monitor the students' out-of-school practice carefully to insure progress. A practice record works well here (see page 144).

3. Two thirty-minute heterogeneous classes per week. Mixing all the beginning brass instruments together becomes a difficult format through which to learn, since each instrument has its special problems of clefs, fingering, slide positions, holding positions, range, care and maintenance, etc. This format works extremely well for older high-school or college students, whose class can be transformed after a few weeks into a brass chamber ensemble. However, it is difficult to use with younger students who remain at the rudimentary level for a longer time. The format does at least have the advantage of students meeting with the instructor twice a week.

4. One thirty-minute heterogeneous class per week. This is the least desirable format to use with beginning brass students. Unfortunately, it is also the one most commonly used in the public schools. The format has too many disadvantages to recommend its use: little help available for the individual, unrelated performance problems mixed together, poor techniques allowed to develop, not enough supervised performance, etc. The argument is often advanced that though this format is weak, it is "better than nothing!" It may not be. Too many students are discouraged by the inherent obstacles in this format.[6] In fact, a student who fails with his beginning instrument performance may have a more negative attitude toward music than one who never got involved in the first place.

FIRST LESSONS FOR BEGINNING BRASS PLAYERS

The first few lessons for any instrument are the most critical and the most difficult to teach. They establish the basic performance concepts for the instrument and the student's basic attitudes toward the instrument, as well. The most competent teacher should handle the first few lessons.

Format

The teacher must have a definite format for starting each of the brass instruments. The following format is recommended:

1. Lip buzzing
2. Mouthpiece placement
3. Mouthpiece buzzing
4. Instrument assembly and disassembly drill
5. Instrument-holding positions
6. Instrument beginning tones
7. Harmonic studies
8. Harmonics and second valve or second slide position

[6]Sidney J. Lawrence and Nadia Dachinger, "Factors Relating to Carryover of Music Training into Adult Life," *Journal of Research in Music Education*, Spring, 1967, p. 29.

9. Harmonics and first valve or third slide position
10. Harmonics and alternating first and second valves or second and third slide positions
11. Improvisation with harmonics, first valve, second valve, or harmonics (first positions), second position, third position
12. Harmonics and first and second valve combination or fourth position
13. Harmonics and second and third valve combination or fifth position
14. Harmonics and first and third valve combination or sixth position
15. Harmonics and first, second, and third valve combination or seventh position
16. Basic care and maintenance of the instrument
17. Directions for home study

This format should take several weeks to accomplish. In any case, there are several important reasons to avoid starting a player with a traditional method book:

First, few method books, if any, follow the principles of brass-instrument performance that are based on harmonics. Instead, traditional method books emphasize scales and key relationships.

Second, more dramatically, the effectiveness of the Suzuki method has shown how important it is for beginners to explore their instruments by sound rather than the printed page.

Third, students have a tendency to devote their whole attention toward trying to learn the music notation and directions while ignoring the sounds they are making.

PREVENTING DROPOUTS

It is discouraging to both the student and the teacher when the student drops out of instrumental music. The student is usually left with a poor attitude toward music and an uncomfortable feeling toward himself or herself. Therefore, teachers should do their best to prevent dropouts.

Many teachers maintain a rule that no student may drop out of the instrumental program until the end of the year. This holds lazy students or those who are easily discouraged by a challenge for the duration, but the teachers are still faced with students dropping out at the end of the year. Here are some of the more common reasons students have given for dropping out of instrumental music.[7]

Instrument Difficult to Play

Most students stated that they dropped out of instrumental music because they found the instrument difficult to play. However, the lack of daily practice probably greatly contributed to these students finding their instruments too difficult. As with learning a foreign language, a student who doesn't incorporate one week's vocabulary into his daily usage will be lost the following week when new vocabulary is introduced. The pacing, sequence, and format of the classes influence the learning of an instrument, as well as the class size, availability of individual help, and the teacher's opinion of the student.

Loss of Interest

There is something definitely wrong with an instrumental music program when many students drop out for loss of interest. Music is potentially one of the most interesting subjects in the entire curriculum, and most students begin their instrumental studies with great interest and enthusiasm. We should, therefore, carefully examine what turns this enthusiasm off. Are we making unreasonable demands on the students' abilities? Are we imposing too much of our taste, values, and goals? Is the music we play really of interest to them?

[7]George Duerksen, *Teaching Instrumental Music* (Washington, D. C.: Music Educators National Conference, 1972), pp. 23-25.

Other Reasons for Dropping Out

Some of the other reasons given by students for dropping out of the instrumental program are: dislike for the teacher, illness, and finances.[8]

PRACTICE RECORDS

Most of the progress or lack of progress students achieve in learning an instrument can be directly attributable to their out-of-class practice habits. Teachers should insist on a daily record of out-of-class practice for each student. The following is an example of a practice record form used successfully by many school districts.

DAILY PRACTICE RECORD

Musician's Name _____ Class _____

Note: Learning to play a musical instrument requires DAILY practice. Try to set aside a definite place and time for practicing each day. Mark your practice record every day and have a parent sign at the end of the week. We suggest *20 to 30 minutes minimum daily practice.*

Week beginning	Mon.	Tues.	Wed.	Thurs.	Fri.	Optional Sat. Sun.	Parent's signature

[8]Anthony J. Martignetti, "Causes of Elementary Instrumental Music Drop Outs," *Journal of Research in Music Education,* Vol. 13, Fall, 1965, pp. 117-183.

Appendix A

SUPPLEMENTARY BRASS
CHAMBER MUSIC ENSEMBLE SELECTIONS

1. Franz Gruber, *Silent Night*
2. Anonymous, *O Come, All Ye Faithful*
3. Anonymous, *Home on the Range*

SILENT NIGHT

Franz Gruber (1818)

O COME, ALL YE FAITHFUL

18th Century Carol

HOME ON THE RANGE

Anonymous
Arr. by Jay Zorn

Appendix B
FINGERING AND SLIDE POSITION CHARTS

CHROMATIC SCALE FINGERING CHART*

Trumpet/Cornet in B♭

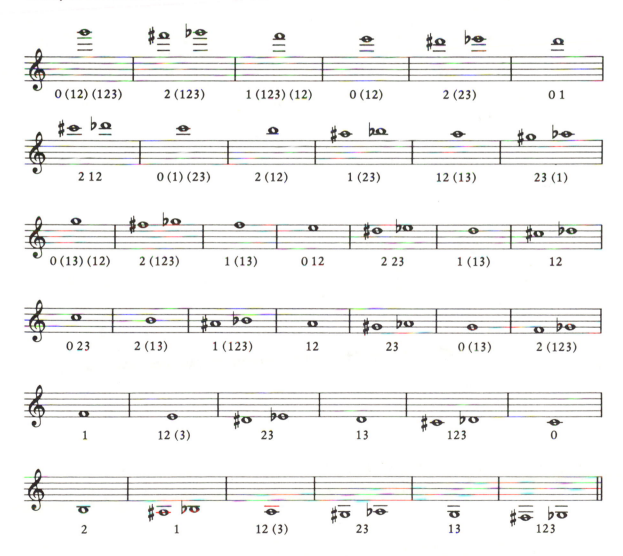

*The best fingerings are listed first. Fingerings in parentheses are possible, but are generally poor in tone quality and intonation. More fingerings are possible in the upper register than appear here.

CHROMATIC SCALE FINGERING CHART*

Horn in F

0 1   12 2 (0)   0 (12) (2)   2 (1)   1 (12)   12 (23)

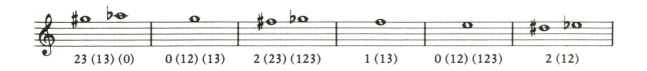

23 (13) (0)   0 (12) (13)   2 (23) (123)   1 (13)   0 (12) (123)   2 (12)

0 1 (13)   2 12   0 (1) (23)   2 (12)   1 (23)   12 (3)

23 (1)   0 (13)   2 (123)   1   0 (12)   2 (23)   1 (13)

(12 (123)   0 (23)   2   1   12 (3)   23   0 (13)

2   1   12   23   13   123

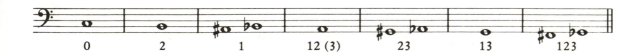

0   2   1   12 (3)   23   13   123

*The best fingerings are listed first. Fingerings in parentheses are possible, but are generally poor in tone quality and intonation. More fingerings are possible in the upper register than appear here.

CHROMATIC SCALE FINGERING CHART*

Horn in B♭*

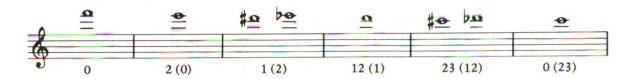

0   2 (0)   1 (2)   12 (1)   23 (12)   0 (23)

2 (23) (1)   1 (12)   12 (0)   23 (2)   0 (1) (13)   2 (12)

0 (1) (23)   2 (12)   1 (23) (1)   12   23 (123)   0 (12) (13)

2 (23)   1   12   23   2   1 (13)   12

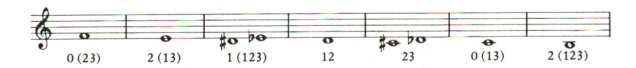

0 (23)   2 (13)   1 (123)   12   23   0 (13)   2 (123)

1   12   23   13   123   0

2   1   12   23   13   123

*The best fingerings are listed first. Fingerings in parentheses are possible, but are generally poor in tone quality and intonation. More fingerings are possible in the upper register than appear here.

**B♭ horn and F-B♭ double horn parts are notated for the F horn and sound a perfect fifth lower than printed.

155

CHROMATIC SCALE SLIDE POSITION CHART*

Trombone (plus F attachment)*

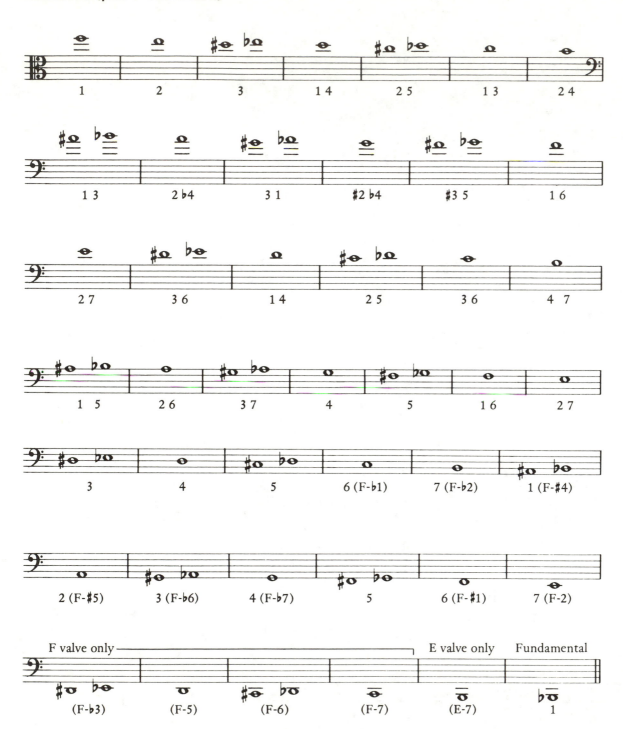

*Basic positions are listed first. The best alternate positions are listed next. The basic positions appear in simplified form. Many more positions than the basic seven are actually used in order to play the notes in tune.

**The F attachment is frequently used by intermediate and advanced students. The extra E valve, however, is available only on expensive professional-quality instruments.

CHROMATIC SCALE FINGERING CHART*

Baritone Horn (four valves)**

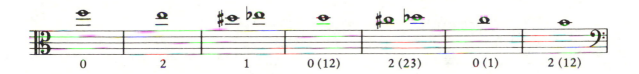

0   2   1   0 (12)   2 (23)   0 (1)   2 (12)

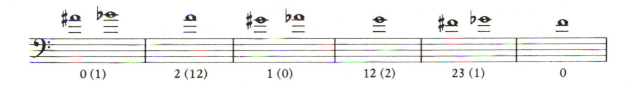

0 (1)   2 (12)   1 (0)   12 (2)   23 (1)   0

2   1   0 (12)   2 (23)   1   12

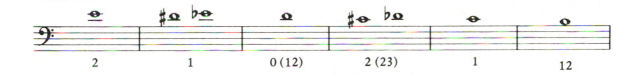

0 (23)   2   1   12 (3)   23   0   2

1   12   23   4 13   24 123   0

2   1   12   23   4 13   24 123

hardly playable ⌐————————————¬

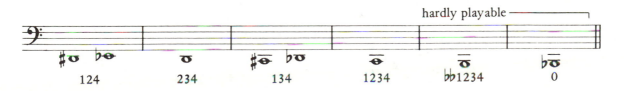

124   234   134   1234   ♭♭1234   ♭0

*The best fingerings are listed first. Fingerings in parentheses are possible, but are generally poor in tone quality and intonation. More fingerings are possible in the upper register than appear here.

**The fourth valve is often found on intermediate and advanced student instruments and greatly aids in correcting some of the lower-register intonation problems.

CHROMATIC SCALE FINGERING CHART*

Tuba in E♭ (three valves)

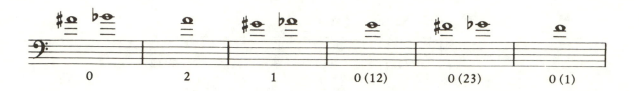

0   2   1   0 (12)   0 (23)   0 (1)

2 (12)   0 (1)   2 (12)   1 (123)   12 (3)   23 (1)

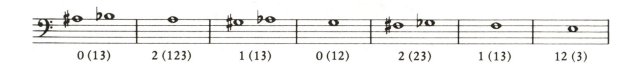

0 (13)   2 (123)   1 (13)   0 (12)   2 (23)   1 (13)   12 (3)

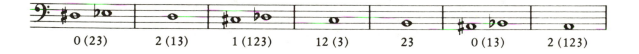

0 (23)   2 (13)   1 (123)   12 (3)   23   0 (13)   2 (123)

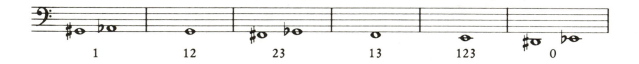

1   12   23   13   123   0

2   1   12   23   13   123

*The best fingerings are listed first. Fingerings in parentheses are possible, but are generally poor in tone quality and intonation. More fingerings are possible in the upper register than appear here.

CHROMATIC SCALE FINGERING CHART*

Tuba in BB♭ (four valves)

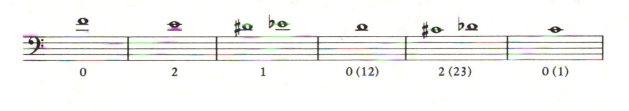

| 0 | 2 | 1 | 0 (12) | 2 (23) | 0 (1) |

| 2 (12) | 0 (1) | 2 (12) | 1 (0) | 12 (3) | 23 (1) |

| 0 (13) | 2 (123) | 1 (13) | 0 12 | 2 (23) | 1 (13) |

| 12 (123) | 0 (23) | 2 (13) | 1 (123) | 12 (3) | 23 |

| 0 (13) | 2 | 1 | 12 (3) | 23 | 13 |

| 123 | 0 | 2 | 1 | 12 | 23 |

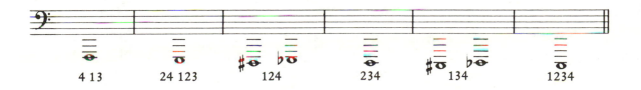

| 4 13 | 24 123 | 124 | 234 | 134 | 1234 |

*The best fingerings are listed first. Fingerings in parentheses are possible, but are generally poor in tone quality and intonation. More fingerings are possible in the upper register than appear here.

Appendix C
BASIC MAJOR AND MINOR SCALES

Trumpet and Horn

BASIC MAJOR SCALES (One Octave)

BASIC MELODIC MINOR SCALES (One Octave)

BASIC CHROMATIC SCALE (One Octave)

Trombone and Baritone Horn

BASIC MAJOR SCALES (One Octave)

BASIC MELODIC MINOR SCALES (One Octave)

BASIC CHROMATIC SCALE (One Octave)

Tuba

BASIC MAJOR SCALES (One Octave)

164

BASIC MELODIC MINOR SCALES (One Octave)

G minor

C minor

F minor

B♭ minor

D minor

A minor

E minor

B minor

F♯ minor

BASIC CHROMATIC SCALE (One Octave)

Appendix D
SELECTED INSTRUCTIONAL MATERIAL
AND SOLO LITERATURE

TRUMPET/CORNET

Instructional Materials

Easy to medium difficulty:

Christopher-Van Bodegraven, *Adventures in Cornet-Trumpet Playing* (Staff Music Publishers)
Clodomir-Foveau, *Petits Exercises* (M. Baron; Elkan-Vogal)
Pease, *Universal's Fundamental Method* (Universal Music Publishers)

Medium to advanced difficulty:

Arban, *Complete Celebrated Method* (Carl Fischer)
Charlier, *Études Transcendantes* (Luduc)
Chavanne, *Études de Virtuosite* (Luduc)
Clarke, *Technical Studies* (Carl Fischer)
Gatti, *Grand Method* (Carl Fischer)
Schlossberg, *Daily Drills and Technical Studies* (M. Baron)
Smith, *Lip Flexibilities* (Carl Fischer)
Zorn, *Exploring the Trumpet's Upper Register* (Kendor)

Solo Literature

Easy to medium difficulty:

Bach-Kent, *Arioso* (Carl Fischer)
Johnson, *Land of Enchantment* (Belwin)
Purcell, *Two Airs* (Mercury)
Strauss-Walters, *Allerseelen* (Rubank)
Williams, *Little Classics Collection* (Charles Colin)

Medium to advanced difficulty:

Anderson, *Trumpeter's Lullaby* (Mills Music)
Balay, *Petite Pièce Concertante* (Southern)
Balay, *Prelude and Ballade* (Belwin)
Burke, *Magic Trumpet* (Carl Fischer)
Clarke, *Celebrated Solos* (Carl Fischer)
Enesco, *Légende* (International)
Giannini, *Concerto* (Remick)

Goedicke, *Concert Etude* (Leeds)
Purcell, *Sonata* (King)
Reed, *Ode for Trumpet* (Hansen)
Ropartz, *Andante and Allegro* (Southern)
Stevens, *Sonata* (Peters)
Wal-Berg, *Concerto for Trumpet* (Leeds)

HORN

Instructional Materials

Easy to medium difficulty:
Franz, *Complete Method* (Carl Fischer)
Hauser, *Foundation to Horn Playing* (Carl Fischer)
Horner, *Primary Studies* (Elkan-Vogal)
Howe, *Method for French Horn* (Remick)

Medium to advanced difficulty:
Kopprasch, *Sixty Selected Studies* (International)
Maxime-Alphonse, *Études* (Luduc)
Pottag, *Preparatory Melodies to Solo Playing* (Belwin)
Pottag-Hovey, *Method for Horn* (Belwin)

Solo Literature

Easy to medium difficulty:
Franck-Boyd, *Panis Angelicus* (Witmark)
Godard-Hauser, *Berceuse* (Carl Fischer)
Lotzenheiser, *Autumn Dream* (Belwin)

Medium to advanced difficulty:
Bach, *Lament* (Edition Musicus)
Block, *Chant D'Amour* (Belwin)
Corelli, *Sonata in G Minor* (Edition Musicus)
Glazounov, *Reverie* (Leeds)
Glière, *Nocturne* (Leeds)
Haydn, *Concerti Nos. 1 and 2* (Boosey & Hawkes)
Mozart, *Concerti Nos. 1, 2, 3, and 4* (Associated)
Scriabin, *Romance* (MCA)
Strauss, *Concerto No. 1* (Carl Fischer)
Strauss, *Concerto No. 2* (Boosey & Hawkes)

TROMBONE

Instructional Materials

Easy to medium difficulty:
Arban-Prescott, *First and Second Year* (Carl Fischer)
Christopher-Van Bodergraven, *Adventures in Trombone Playing* (Staff)
Long, *Elementary Method* (Rubank)

Medium to advanced difficulty:
Arban, *Complete Method* (Carl Fischer)
Blazevitch, *Twenty-Six Melodious Studies* (Am-Rus)
Blume, *Thirty-Six Studies for Trombone* (Carl Fischer)
Cimera, *Two Hundred Twenty-One Progressive Studies for the Trombone* (Belwin)
Clarke, *Method for Trombone* (Carl Fischer)
Lafosse, *Complete Method for Trombone* (Leduc)
Marsteller, *Advanced Slide Technique* (Southern)
Ostrander, *The F Attachment and the Bass Trombone* (Charles Colin)
Rochut, *Melodious Etudes* (Carl Fischer)
Schlossberg, *Daily Drills and Technical Studies* (Baron)
Tyrrell, *Forty Progressive Studies* (Boosey & Hawkes)

Solo Literature

Easy to medium difficulty:
Adams, *Holy City* (Embassy)
Barat, *Andante et Allegro* (Cundy-Bettoney)
Bohm, *Italian Romance* (Carl Fischer)
Elgar, *Land of Hope and Glory* (Boosey & Hawkes)
Fauré, *The Palms* (Cundy-Bettoney)
Haydn, "Adagio" from *Cello Concerto* (Witmark)
Saint-Saëns, *My Heart at thy Sweet Voice* (Cundy-Bettoney)

Medium to advanced difficulty:
Bozza, *Ballade* (Co-Di)
Galliard, *Sonatas* (McGinnis & Marx)
Guilmant, *Morçeau Symphonique* (Remick)
Handel-Marsteller, *Concerto* (Southern)
Hindemith, *Sonata* (AMP)
Pryor, *Blue Bells of Scotland* (Carl Fischer)
Rimsky-Korsakov, *Concerto* (International)
Sanders, *Sonata for Trombone* (Remick)
Stevens, *Sonatina* (Peer)
Weber, *Romanza Appassionata* (Carl Fischer)

BARITONE HORN

Instructional Materials

Easy to medium difficulty:
Beeler, *Baritone Method* (MPHC)
Christopher-Van Bodegraven, *Adventures in Baritone Playing* (Staff)
Skornica-Boltz, *Intermediate Method* (Rubank)

Medium to advanced difficulty:
Arban, *Complete Method* (Carl Fischer)
Archimede, *Foundation to Baritone Playing* (Carl Fischer)
Rochut, *Melodious Etudes* (Carl Fischer)
Schlossberg, *Daily Drills and Technical Studies* (Baron)
Voxman, *Selected Studies* (Rubank)

Solo Literature

Easy to medium difficulty:
    Berlioz, *Recitative and Prayer* (Presser)
    Chopin-Marsteller, *Nocturne* (Southern)
    Haydn, "Adagio" from *Cello Concerto* (Witmark)
    Smith, *The Challenger* (Belwin)

Medium to advanced difficulty:
    Alary, *Morçeau de Concours* (Carl Fischer)
    Barat, *Introduction and Dance* (Baron)
    Clarke, *Maid of the Mist* (Carl Fischer)
    Guilmant, *Morçeau Symphonique* (International)
    Marcello, *Sonata in G Minor* (International)
    Weber, *Romanza Appassionata* (Carl Fischer)

TUBA

Instructional Materials

Easy to medium difficulty:
    Arban-Prescott, *First and Second Year for Tuba* (Carl Fischer)
    Beeler, *Tuba Method* (Remick)
    Bell, *Foundations to Tuba Playing* (Carl Fischer)
    Clarke, *Elementary Method for Tuba* (Mills)
    Skornica-Boltz, *Intermediate Method* (Rubank)

Medium to advanced difficulty:
    Arban, *Complete Method* (Carl Fischer)
    Bell, *Daily Routines* (Charles Colin)
    Bernard, *Forty Studies* (Luduc)
    Geib, *The Geib Method for Tuba* (Carl Fischer)
    Vlasiliev, *Twenty-Four Melodious Etudes* (Leeds)

Solo Literature

Easy to medium difficulty:
    Bach-Bell, *Gavotte* (Carl Fischer)
    Bell, *Jolly Jumbo* (Belwin)
    Peter-Bell, *The Jolly Coppersmith* (Belwin)
    Weber, *The Elephant Dance* (Belwin)

Medium to advanced difficulty:
    Bach-Bell, *Air and Bourrée* (Carl Fischer)
    Bernstein, *Waltz for Mippy III* (G. Schirmer)
    Beversdorf, *Sonata* (Southern)
    Hartley, *Sonatina* (Elkan-Vogel)
    Hindemith, *Sonata* (Schott)
    Lebedev, *Allegro de Concert* (Presser)
    Persichetti, *Serenade No. 12* (Elkan-Vogel)
    Tcherepnine, *Andante* (Boosey & Hawkes)
    Vaughan Williams, *Concerto* (Oxford)

Appendix E
SELECTED READINGS

Amstutz, A. K., "A Videofluorographic Study of the Teeth Aperture, Instrument Pivot and Tongue Arch and Their Influence on Trumpet Performance." Doctoral dissertation, University of Oklahoma, 1970.

Bach, Vincent, *The Art of Trumpet Playing.* Available from The Selmer Company, Elkhart, Ind.

———, *Mouthpiece and Embouchure Manual.* Available from The Selmer Company, Elkhart, Ind.

Bellamah, Joseph L., *Brass Facts: A Survey of Teaching and Playing Methods of Leading Brass Authorities.* San Antonio, Texas: Southern Music Company, 1960.

Bouhuys, A., "Lung Volumes and Breathing Patterns in Wind-Instrument Players," *Journal of Applied Physiology,* Vol. 19, No. 5, 1964.

Briggs, G. V., "Electrophysiological Examination of Labial Function in College-Age Trumpet Performers." Doctoral dissertation, University of Oklahoma, 1968.

Bush, Irving, *Artistic Trumpet Technique.* Hollywood, Calif.: Highland Music Company, 1962.

Carse, Adam, *Musical Wind Instruments.* London: Macmillan and Company, Ltd., 1939.

Carter, W., "The Role of the Glottis in Brass Playing," *The Instrumentalist: Brass Anthology,* 1969.

Colin, Charles, *The Brass Player.* New York: Charles Colin, 1972.

Duerksen, George L., *Teaching Instrumental Music.* Washington, D. C.: Music Educators National Conference, 1972.

Farkas, Philip, *The Art of Brass Playing.* Bloomington, Ind.: Wind Music, Inc., 1962.

———, *The Art of French Horn Playing.* Evanson, Ill.: Summy-Birchard Company, 1956.

Faulkner, M. E., "Reports upon European Research in Breathing for Wind Instruments," *The Brass World,* Vol. 1, No. 1, 1965.

Faulkner, M. E. and S. Horvath, "Measurement of Heart Volume and the Results of an Electrocardiogram During Blowing of a Trumpet Mouthpiece," *The Brass World,* Vol. 3, No. 2, 1967.

Faulkner, M. E. and E. P. Sharpey-Schafer, "Circulatory Effects of Trumpet Playing," *British Medical Journal,* Vol. 1, 1959.

Fennell, Frederick, *Time and the Winds.* Kenosha, Wis.: G. Leblanc Corp., 1954.

Hall, J. C., "A Radiographic, Spectographic, and the Photographic Study of the Non-Labial Physical Changes Which Occur in the Transition from Middle to Low and Middle to High Registers During Trumpet Performance." Doctoral dissertation, Indiana University, 1954.

Hanson, F., *Brass Playing, Mechanism and Technique.* New York: Carl Fischer, Inc., 1968.

Haynie, J. J., *A Videofluorographic Presentation of the Physiological Phenomena Influencing Trumpet Performance.* Denton, Texas: School of Music, North Texas State University, 1967.

Henderson, H. W., "An Experimental Study of Trumpet Embouchure," *The Journal of the Acoustical Society of America,* Vol. 13, 1942.

Hiigel, L. E., "The Relationship of Syllables to Pitch and Tonguing in Brass Instrument Playing." Doctoral dissertation, University of California, 1967.

Isley, C. L., "Facial Muscles in Brass Embouchure." Unpublished manuscript, Appalachian State University, 1971.

Kleinhammer, Edward, *The Art of Trombone Playing.* Evanston, Ill.: Summy-Birchard Company, 1963.

Knaub, Donald, *Trombone Teaching Techniques.* Fairport, N. Y.: Rochester Music Publishers.

Leno, H. L., "Lip Vibration Characteristics of Selected Trombone Performers." Doctoral dissertation, University of Arizona, 1970.

Martin, D. W., "Lip Vibration in a Cornet Mouthpiece," *The Journal of the Acoustical Society of America,* Vol. 13, 1942.

Meidt, J. A., "A Cinefluorographic Investigation of Oral Adjustments for Various Aspects of Brass Instrument Performance." Doctoral dissertation, University of Iowa, 1967.

Merriman, L. C., *A Study to Explore the Possible Uses of X-Ray Motion Picture Photography for the Improvement of Brass Instrument Teaching, USDHEW Rep. No. BR-6-8322.* Washington, D. C.: United States Government Printing Office, 1967.

Merriman, L. C. and J. A. Meidt, "A Cinefluorographic Investigation of Brass Instrument Performance," *Journal of Research in Music Education,* Vol. 16, No. 1, Spring, 1968.

Nichols, R. L., F. Hanson, W. A. Daehling, and H. Hofman, *The Improvement of Brass Instrument Teaching Through the Use of a Profile of the Physical Aspects Involved, USDHEW Rep. No. BR-0H-008.* Washington, D. C.: United States Government Printing Office, 1971.

Noble, Clyde E., *The Psychology of Cornet and Trumpet Playing.* Missoula, Mont.: The Mountain Press, 1964.

Reinhardt, Donald S., *Pivot System Series.* Philadelphia, Pa.: Elkan-Vogel Company, Inc., 1942.

Richtmeyer, L. C., "A Definite Analysis of Brass Embouchure Abnormalities Including Recommended Remedial Techniques." Doctoral dissertation, Michigan University, 1966.

Schuller, Gunther, *Horn Technique.* New York: Oxford University Press, 1962.

Schwartz, H. L., *The Story of Musical Instruments.* Elkhart, Ind.: C. G. Conn Company, 1938.

Severinsen, C., *Clinic Notes for Brass Teachers.* Elkhorn, Wis.: Getzen Company, Inc., n.d.

Trosper, O. W., "The Principles and Practice of Producing Vibrato in Brass Instrument Performance." Doctoral dissertation, Columbia University, 1962.

Weast, Robert D., *Brass Performance: An Analytical Text.* New York: McGinnis & Marx, 1966.

_____, "A Stroboscopic Analysis of Lip Function," *The Instrumentalist: Brass Anthology,* Vol. 18, 1969.

Weast, Robert D. and A. Hake, "A Definitive Analysis of Mouthpiece Pressure," *The Brass World,* Vol. 1, No. 2, 1965.

Winter, James H., *The Brass Instruments.* Boston, Mass.: Allyn & Bacon, Inc., 1969.

Zorn, Jay D., *Exploring the Trumpet's Upper Register.* Delevan, N. Y.: Kendor Music, Inc., 1975.

INDEX